Dreaming of Italy

Las Vegas and the Virtual Grand Tour

Dreaming of Italy

Las Vegas and the Virtual Grand Tour

Text by Giovanna Franci
Photographs by Federico Zignani
Afterword by José Gamez

University of Nevada Press
Reno & Las Vegas

University of Nevada Press
Reno, Nevada 89557 USA

Bononia University Press
Via Zamboni 25 – 40126 Bologna (Italy)
www.buponline.com

All photographs, unless otherwise credited, have been taken especially for this book by Federico Zignani.

Photos 12, 14, and 88 courtesy of Bellagio Hotel and Casino (Russell MacMasters); photo 38 courtesy of Thyssen-Bornemisza Collection, Madrid, Spain; photo 75 courtesy of Vatican Museums, Rome, Vatican City; photo 36 courtesy of Venetian Civic Museums, Doge's Palace Museum, Venice, Italy; and photos 153 and 154 courtesy of The Venetian Resort Hotel Casino, Las Vegas.

Translated by Debra Lyn Christie

ISBN 0-87417-610-7

Graphic designer and page make up: Gianluca Bollina

First printing: January 2005
Printed in Italy by Officine Grafiche Litosei s.r.l.

To our family (Flavio, Ines, Gabriella, Ubaldo, Leonardo, Nicola, Anna, Gabriele, Lidia, Dario), and in memory of Lea, forever Ladybug

Las Vegas: Bellagio Hotel, Overall View

Las Vegas: Caesars Palace, Chariot, Detail

Contents

Acknowledgments

Our sincere gratitude to the many friends and colleagues, scholars and collectors, librarians and representatives of institutions, archives, firms, and properties who have provided precious material, ready assistance, and information in the compilation of this book.

Particular thanks to: Grand Hotel Villa Serbelloni, Bellagio, Lake Como, Italy (Antonio Calzolaro, Reservation Manager); Grand Hotel Villa d'Este, Cernobbio, Lake Como (Claudio Ceccherelli, General Manager, and Annamaria Duvia, Public Relations Manager); Caesars Palace, Las Vegas (Michael Coldwell, Director, Public Relations, Park Place Entertainment now Caesars Entertainment, Inc.); The Forum Shops at Caesars, Las Vegas (Kristina Steinbach, Marketing & Tourism Coordinator); Bellagio Hotel and Casino, Las Vegas (Angela R. Torres, Public Relations Coordinator, and Christi Bragington, Public Relations Specialist, MGM Mirage); The Venetian Resort-Hotel-Casino, Las Vegas (Joe Ham, former Public Relations Manager, and Scott J. Messinger, Vice President of Brand Marketing); The Grove, Caruso Affiliated Holdings, Los Angeles, Calif. (Jennifer Gordon, Director of Marketing and Tourism); Megan Becker-Leckrone; Piero Casadei; Robert Casillo; Arlene Cattani-Howard; Cesare Cesarini; Alessandra di Luzio; Guido Fink; Gabriele Franci; Bernard Frischer; José Gamez; Marino Golinelli; Emiliano Guevara; Paul Holdengräber; Franco La Polla; Maria Gabriella Mazzocchi; Giancarlo Piretti; David Quint; Gia and Giovanni Rigotti; John Paul Russo; Laura Salvini; Gino Scatasta; Michael Serwatka; Guido Sesani; Nathan Shapira; Ester Zago; Flavio Zignani.

1. Introduction: Las Vegas and the Postmodern Grand Tour

The term "Grand Tour" usually means "travels taken between the sixteenth and the nineteenth centuries, first by generations of European aristocrats and bourgeois, and then by Americans."[1] These travels had a multifaceted goal: a journey of both knowledge and pleasure. They also had a clearly formative purpose linked to the rite of initiation, to the passage from adolescence to maturity: a Coming of Age for upper-class youth, but also the sentimental journey of Pre-Romantic and Romantic artists who descended from Northern Europe toward the shores of the Mediterranean Sea, attracted by the mild climate of "Il Bel Paese" and the Fine Arts.

> *"In one's imagination, Italy has been and will always be the land of sun and song; and neither storms, nor rain, nor snow will ever cool the enthusiasm that the word Italy sparks in every poetic soul."*
>
> *Henry W. Longfellow*

1. Bellagio, Lake Como, Italy: with the Pre-Alps in the Background

Foreign visitors discovered the most memorable places in Italy – places that Italians themselves weren't even aware of – from the lakes of Lombardy (fig. 1) to Venice (fig. 2), to the *villas* of the Veneto; from Rome (fig. 3) and the *Campagna romana*, to Naples and the Amalfi Coast, from the Ligurian Riviera to the hill towns of Umbria and Tuscany. The reason for this fascination, which is still echoed in modern travel to Italy, is the unique fusion of artwork and landscape, and that special atmosphere that the name Italy evokes. It is an Italy that is often only imagined, whose overwhelming charm, often somewhat lapsed, can still bewitch foreigners. One might even say that the phenomenon of the Grand Tour still continues, though it may have changed (because the various kinds of travelers and their travel habits have changed) from travel for the elite few, inviting adventure and discovery, to organized travel, typical of modern mass tourism.

2. Venice, Italy: Lagoon with Gondolas

The main aim of this book is to follow two parallel and closely intertwined topics. First, going back to the model of the Grand Tour, we will attempt to uncover the cause for a particular phase in the recent evolution of Las Vegas: the emergence of Italian-themed mega-resort casinos. Secondly, we will briefly cover the stages of transformation that Las Vegas – emblem of the renewed American dream – has undergone: from a city dedicated to gambling, to a Disneyland-like theme park, to what is now a mandatory destination for tourists at the end/beginning of a millennium, and finally to a broader cultural center.

What type of "communication system" does Las Vegas represent today? If, according to a widely shared opinion, it has become a giant theme park, then the "theme" is primarily that of European cities, and to paraphrase Marshall McLuhan, we could thus say that the sign/theme is the message.

It is from this perspective that, through discussion on the relationship between original and copy, this book intends to exhibit variations on the "Italian theme" in three chosen examples of resort-casinos on the Las Vegas Strip. And so Caesars Palace (fig. 4), the Bellagio (fig. 5), and The Venetian (fig. 6) will be compared with their imitated models, or

3. Rome, Italy: Roman Forum

4. *Las Vegas: Caesars Palace, Exterior with Temple and Columns*

5. *Las Vegas: Bellagio Hotel, View of Lake and "Village"*

6. Las Vegas: The Venetian Hotel, Gondola and Canals

the "originals" – Rome, Bellagio on Lake Como, and Venice – while the Grand Tour scheme will serve as a frame for the play between imitation and/or reinvention.

This complex dynamic of exchange is why Las Vegas has been singled out as the gaudiest icon of modern travel, the epitome of a process of globalization by which cities, duplicated according to the "urban theme park" model, seem to be copies of each other. In fact, the city of Las Vegas can be seen, both in its urban appearance and in its gaming and economic attractions, as a sought-after destination in a "pilgrimage" of our times. It is, in terms of social diffusion and importance (in a mass consumer and technological context), a copy of the Grand Tour in Europe, and especially, in Italy. But a trip to Las Vegas also challenges the idea of travel as "real" movement because – in the Internet age – we can go anywhere, in real time, without leaving the Nevada desert: a perfect example of the "virtual" Grand Tour.

"Italian make-believe in the heart of Vegas."

In the panorama of theme architecture, that which has proved most absorbing is the image of Italy in Las Vegas. Why does Europe, and particularly Italy, continue to hold such an exclusive appeal, and not just in Las Vegas? We lately read[2] that Henry Gluck, one of the minds behind Caesars Palace, is building a replica of Florence's Ponte Vecchio over an artificial lake about 15 miles from Las Vegas, while a resort called the Siena, publicized as "A Touch of Tuscany on the River," recently arose in the competing city of Reno. In Atlantic City, the Borgata is currently under construction – yet another reinvention of an Italian village inspired by the Bellagio and The Venetian. And it doesn't stop there. Another example, not just outside

Nevada, but outside the United States, is the fascinating, monstrous melange of Italy that is Venus Fort, a shopping mall built on Odaiba, a manmade island in Tokyo Bay, Japan. The name Venus obviously recalls the goddess of love and beauty, but differently from the monothematic hotels in Las Vegas, here one finds a bit of Rome mixed with a touch of Florence, Venice, and Portofino. Once again, a concentrate of the Grand Tour in Italy.

The Italian label is undoubtedly popular in America, from fashion to cooking; in the collective imagination of tourists, the "Italy" theme is synonymous with elegance, refined taste, decorum, in a word, beauty, but also with leisure, breakaway behavior (gambling), sexuality (decadence). It is also synonymous with countries that are exotic and familiar at the same time, countries seen as places for the elite, testimony of the cultural leap for those who know them, or even for those who have barely heard of them. New visitors to Las Vegas do not just go to gamble in the casinos. They also go to see the phantasmagoria of the most recent constructions: for example, some go to The Venetian because they have already seen the real Venice, or because they are willing to settle for the surrogate. Sometimes it is even possible to speak of cultural travel, where the "pedagogic" intent that characterized the original Grand Tour seems to be making a return.

So the Peninsula once more becomes not so much the preferred destination as the preferred theme. Venice, with its lagoon and gondolas, Bellagio and Lake Como reflecting colorful villages on its waters, the sunny Riviera, the mighty monuments of the Eternal City: everything can be enjoyed in one place, in the middle of the Nevada desert. As we have said, the pattern is that of the copy, which often results in something more real than the real thing, according to the principle of concentration, or miniaturization. However, in the chosen examples, treatment of the copy undergoes significant variations according not only to the intentions of the casino owners and architects, but also to the use by the public that visits them.

But there is more: each site, reproduced in the resort hotel-casino theme, is seen as a laboratory of contemporary architectural design whereby creative and fanciful imitation comes together in a playful combination of styles. The result is the paradoxical creation of an "original" through repetition or, in other words, new originals obtained through copies.

In this journey/pilgrimage our guide has been a book, *Learning from Las Vegas: The Forgotten Symbolism of Architectural Form,* by architects Robert Venturi, Denise Scott Brown, and Steven Izenour. First published in 1972, it is recognized as a classic of postmodern aesthetics. In this accurate and extraordinarily perceptive study of Las Vegas architecture in the late sixties, the three architects identify a new phenomenon in contemporary design: specifically, the rejection of that austere and rigorous modernist architecture for which "form is function," in favor of an architecture that stresses signs and symbols, with no distinction between high culture and popular culture. Las Vegas offers an ideal multidimensional system of signs, from gigantic billboards and neon decorations that cover the façades of hotel-casinos, bringing the Strip's multicolored night to life, to theme hotels of the latest generation, which are themselves, taken as a whole, meaningful signs. It is an architecture that makes use of popular and commercial language, an architecture that unites the most varied themes in American culture with the exotic mythology of the most fantastic oases of pleasure. Following a principle of inclusion and allusion, this architecture creates the image of a city that is both concrete and evocative.

In the case of Las Vegas, even the three American architects return to the model of the Grand Tour and don't hesitate to compare the *piazzas* (fig. 7) of Rome to the Strip and its Caesars Palace (fig. 8): "In the eighteenth and nineteenth centuries an integral part of an architect's education consisted of sketching Roman ruins. If the eighteenth-century architect discovered his design gestalt by means of the Grand Tour and a sketch pad, we as twentieth-century architects will have to find our own 'sketch pad' for Las Vegas."[3]

The happy choice of the book's title, *Learning from Las Vegas,* is no accident. Las Vegas still has much to teach us about the life *in* and *of* the city, about the societies both of today and of tomorrow. We believe that Venturi, Scott Brown, and Izenour were right to ask us to look with different eyes: "A new type of urban form emerging in America and Europe, radically different from that we have known; one we have been ill-equipped to deal with and that, from ignorance, we define today as urban sprawl."[4] That group of daring architects taught us to see in the city street, with its empty façades like film sets that only come alive at night with colorful neon lights, something beyond its aspect as a commercial city of pure entertainment, a loved and hated icon. It becomes a model of America and of the city of the future. We also believe that even Hal Rothman (a professor of history at the University of Nevada, Las Vegas) is correct when he writes that "Las Vegas has become the place where the twenty-first century begins, a center of the postindustrial world. It has become the first spectacle of the postmodern world."[5] From periphery to paradigm: Las Vegas is truly "an All-American City," a chameleon-like city whose identity is continuously remodeled and which presents itself as a script that anyone can rewrite at pleasure.

7. Rome: Pantheon with the Fountain in Piazza della Rotonda, Giacomo della Porta (Second Half of the Sixteenth Century)

8. Las Vegas: Caesars Palace, Colonnade and Pool, Detail

Today there are numerous serious and less serious essays – we can call them "meta-entertainment" – on Las Vegas as "Pleasuredome," "Fantasyland," "Adult Playground," "Disneyland for Adults," "Urban Freak," and "Game Mecca" (carrying the dual meaning of playing and gambling), with all the analogous and interchangeable clichés. Similarly, there are numerous volumes of historical-sociological analyses that speak of the origins and development of the city, the diversity of its population, the entertainment industry, and so on. Less teeming is the shelf dedicated to the urban-architectural aspect, always looked at suspiciously and analyzed superciliously, and to the interior and exterior design of the casinos, no longer in motel style with streamlined façades, but now sumptuous resorts. Even more rare are books analyzing the "post-Venturi" phase with a keen eye, instead of speaking ironically in superficial anecdotes about kitsch casinos elevated to symbols of bad taste, or about the "adultescent" public! It may seem easy to write about Las Vegas, but over the course of this work, it proved more and more difficult.

But to shed light on the complexity of our discourse on Las Vegas, the written commentary (more closely tied to the history of taste and cultural studies than to architecture in a strict sense) is supported by the "visual" language of photography, an integral part of our project. Images flow before our eyes, showing us places as perfect examples of the "old" and the "new" Grand Tour, a juxtaposition of "original" and "fake," for the joy of discovery that must accompany every trip, real or virtual. (figs. 9,10)

9. Venice: Doge's Palace, Detail of Balcony

*10. Las Vegas: The Venetian Hotel,
Doge's Palace, Detail of Balcony*

2. Las Vegas, from Gambling Mecca to Postmodern Icon

"Let's learn to understand, love, and even laugh with what we thought we hated. Long live the big sign and the little building! Long live the building that is a sign! Long live Las Vegas!"
Robert Venturi, Denise Scott Brown, Steven Izenour

The year 2005 will mark the one hundredth anniversary of the birth of Las Vegas, or better, of what was originally just a small townsite with a cluster of saloons and brothels, a supply station between Los Angeles and Salt Lake City, first along a dirt road and later along the railroad line.

But in these hundred years, when exactly did Las Vegas become "Vegas" with its own unmistakable style, the place that Mark Weatherford nostalgically calls a "state of mind" in his book *Cult Vegas?*[6] Las Vegas is and has always been a city of excess and contradictions, "a muddle of emotions, a flash of spectacular ideas, a vortex of spectacles, colors, and sounds…a magnificent, bizarre, opulent mirage in a place teaming with hallucinations par excellence," as Isabella Brega brightly notes.[7]

Our intention here is not to recount the city's history; nor do we intend to make a sociological analysis of its tourism industry and how it has changed over the course of the years.[8] However, a concise summary of what has come to pass in the city's brief but intense life over the last century will serve as a starting point for understanding later transformations. In any case, Las Vegas clearly cannot be shut forever in a cage. It is probable that, even as this book is being printed, the face of the city will undergo still further transformations.

"This is a windy town. People blow in, people blow out."
Victor Mature in Las Vegas Story

In 1907, electric lights lit up Fremont Street, which thus became the first center, now historic, of the future "Neon District." However, it was in the early 1930s, with construction of the Hoover Dam (1931–35) bringing water to the desert valleys, and with the legalization of gambling in the state of Nevada (1931), that the foundations of Las Vegas were established. From that point to the end of the decade, the ease of contracting and dissolving marriages would help to increase the city's fame and riches, beginning with Hollywood star Clark Gable's much-talked-about divorce from Ria Langham in his haste to marry Carole Lombard.[9] It is this "incubation" period that Alan Hess associates with the "protostrip," the first of no less than six phases identified by the scholar between the pioneering era and the 1990s.[10]

In an attempt to draw a simplified map of the architectural-urban development of Las Vegas, a good starting point is the "old western" phase, which recovered, as would the cinema, a specific and unique era in American history, turning it into an epic. And thus the El Rancho arose just outside the city in 1941, and in 1942 was followed by the Last Frontier. With décor halfway between "old Mexico" and "dude ranch," both are *ante litteram* examples of the theme architecture that went on to develop, though in an entirely different way, in more recent phases of the city's history.

The moment of radical change, however, came right after World War II when Cosa Nostra saw in the Nevada gambling market an opportunity to expand its business. The Mob started with the Flamingo, born from the imagination and entrepreneurial skills of Benjamin Siegel, otherwise known as "Bugsy," though the idea for the casino came from his friend Billy Wilkerson. The club opened in 1946, inaugurating a decisive period for Las Vegas hotel-casinos as well as a series of sophisticated motels in modern and streamlined style, looking out onto the Strip. But Bugsy, by then a legendary gangster with Mob ties, would not enjoy the satisfaction of his dream come true for long. Swimming in debt, he was murdered a year later by his "partners" and hence delivered to the mythography on Las Vegas's origins, along with his "fabulous" Flamingo, a sophisticated luxury hotel equipped with elegant suites, a swimming pool, tennis courts, a golf course, and lush gardens.

A new architecture was arising in Las Vegas, a "sleek supper-club architecture" that melded Hollywood atmosphere with the exotic touch of Miami Beach and Havana, and the elegance of Monte Carlo. An attention to detail, from color to materials used for interiors and furnishings, was introduced by this type of hotel-casino, identified under the category of "carpet joints" to distinguish it from the more rustic, less refined "sawdust joints."[11]

In *I.D.: The Magazine of International Design,* Julia Szabo wrote, "New York has its skyline, Venice has its canals, Paris has the Eiffel Tower, Giza has its Sphynx. Las Vegas has all of the above. So what's the single, identifying landmark that says 'You are here' to a weary traveler without a map? The carpeting."[12] Indeed, the importance of detail in the interior décor of these new resort hotel-casinos gave great importance to the harmony and coherence of the whole: the pattern of the carpets in rooms and hallways alike had to match the building, and specific designers were employed to choose the elaborate designs and colors. One example for all: the ballroom in the Bellagio which carries Renaissance-inspired decorations with overtones recalling majolica ceramics by Della Robbia and Italian palazzos. (fig. 11)

Don't, however, be confused by the large size of the resorts from the 1980s and '90s, when the hotels were shaped like tall, thin prisms, often intersecting like stars, with an imaginative theme-based façade. The much smaller hotels of this earlier period were generally designed in a motel or bungalow style and distinguished by a tall, slender sign. The deco, modernist style of Los Angeles had served as a lesson.

Hollywood personalities began linking their names to hotels during the 1950s and '60s, which coincided with the development of the Strip, the television boom, and air conditioning, as well as with nuclear experiments in the desert north of the city. The Desert Inn hosted Frank Sinatra's Las Vegas debut, and the Sands became his usual haunt between 1952 and 1967 for shows by the "Voice" and his friends. The notorious "Rat Pack," consisting of Dean (Dino) Martin, Sammy Davis Jr., Joey Bishop, and Peter

11. Las Vegas: Bellagio Hotel, Halls

Lawford, along with Sinatra, appeared together at the Sands while they were simultaneously working on the 1960 film *Ocean's Eleven*,[13] recently remade starring George Clooney, Brad Pitt, and Julia Roberts.

If many of the hotel-casinos of the era have now either disappeared or changed radically, it is precisely the "ephemeral" art of the cinema that preserves their memory. This is the case for the Sahara, the Riviera, the Desert Inn, the Sands, and the Flamingo, all of which host exploits by our heroes for their great heist. And cinema also documents the end…as a show: Martin Scorsese used the demolition that destroyed the Dunes in 1993 for the ending of *Casino*, while in 1995 Tim Burton used the implosion of the Landmark Hotel for a scene in *Mars Attacks!* Shortly before its 1996 demolition, the Sands, mythical "place in the sun," served as the set for an airplane crash scene in the film *Con Air* (1997). Lastly, though of course not least, the Hacienda Hotel was blown up during the night between 31 December 1996 and 1 January 1997, to welcome the new year in a blaze of fireworks.

All these films are today an important document for historical memory of a Las Vegas which is either largely gone or in continual transformation. They also serve as a cross-section of American life and history. As such, this city, already the copy of copies, further multiplies its image in these cinematic copies, extending from the screen into the global imaginary.

In those years of Strip development, the destinies of three great show business personalities would cross. In addition to the great Frank, Elvis Presley and Howard Hughes would contribute to the city's history. In 1967, when Howard Hughes — one of Ava Gardner's former lovers — bought the Sands, Sinatra left the hotel abruptly. The next year, it was Caesars Palace that billed his show in its Circus Maximus showroom, defining Sinatra as "the noblest Roman of them all." But in the meantime, another "King" had claimed his share of the limelight, and from Sinatra's swing style there was a changeover to (or overlap with) Elvis and rock 'n' roll. After his first show at the New Frontier in 1956, Southern boy Elvis Presley waited until 1969 to return to Las Vegas, with a big show at the International Hotel (the Las Vegas Hilton since 1971). But in a certain sense, the superstar had never left Las Vegas. In 1964, he had starred with Ann-Margret in the popular film *Viva Las Vegas,* in wide-screen Technicolor. The film added to the allure of the "bright-light city" of the 1960s, helping to turn it into an American pop icon, while Elvis's marriage to tender, young Priscilla Beaulieu, in 1967, confirmed his place as star of the gossip columns. From 1969, Elvis's fate was entwined with the city's; he held shows there annually until 1976, one year prior to his premature death amid successes and personal crises, triumphs and physical deterioration, in the end becoming almost a caricature of himself. However, the "King of Memphis" never really died in truth, and not just because of the legend that rears its head every now and then, according to which he willfully left the stage and the world of show business. It is also and above all due to the phenomenon of copying, or rather cloning, to which he is subjected by thousands of replicants throughout the U.S. and Europe, through fan clubs and impersonators who hold periodic conventions. This phenomenon is documented in the 1992 film *Honeymoon in Vegas*, in which a squad of "Flying Elvi" parachute through the Las Vegas skies. What personality better than Elvis represents the phenomenon of fake and forgery that characterizes, for better and worse, the history of Vegas?

Finally, eccentric, rich, and mysterious Hollywood producer Howard Hughes tied both his life and his business to Las Vegas, starting in 1952, when he produced the film *Las Vegas Story*, a drama built to size for the star of the moment, the atomic Jane Russell. However, in 1966 Hughes decided to actually move to the Nevada city, shutting him-

12. Las Vegas: Bellagio Hotel, Night View (*credit: Bellagio Hotel)

self in the Desert Inn penthouse and obsessively trying to buy one hotel after another. The Sands, the Frontier, the Castaways, and the Silver Slipper all became his property. When blocked by antitrust laws, enacted to keep him from obtaining a dangerous monopoly, the magnate decided to abandon Las Vegas in 1970, but not before purchasing the Landmark Hotel as well. He was, in any case, forerunner to enterprising owners and builders such as Kirk Kerkorian in the 1970s, or more recently, Bob Stupak, Steve Wynn, and Sheldon Adelson in the 1980s and 1990s, who sparked the rebirth of Las Vegas. Gangsters of the era of Bugsy and Sinatra are no longer in fashion; the scandals of the casinos had their effect. The new bosses are now the hotel-casino owners/operators, the designers/architects, or even the new generation multinationals.

"Men like Steve Wynn (Mirage/Bellagio), Sheldon Adelson (The Venetian), and Tony Marnell (Rio) are the new Medici of Las Vegas," writes Paul Davies,[14] the Patrons who, like popes and lords in their times, brought the Renaissance to life. And perhaps this seemingly sacrilegious comparison is not even entirely out of place.

> *"We're goin' to Vegas."*
> *"Las Vegas?"*
> *"I don't know any other Vegas."*
> Jon Voight, Lookin' to Get Out

Though Las Vegas has changed, it continues to be known for its heroic phase as the *Neon Metropolis*. And regarding those neon signs considered as "polychrome sculptures," signs and symbols of a unique moment in the city's development, Venturi, Scott Brown, and Izenour wrote many memorable pages. Though much newer than the original building, one sign which escaped destruction is the *porte-cochère* at the Flamingo Hilton, designed in 1976 by the master of neon signs Raul Rodriguez. Inspired by its glow, Tom Wolfe wrote, "Such colors! All the new electrochemical pastels of the Florida littoral: tangerine, broiling magenta, livid pink, incarnadine, fuchsia, demure, Congo ruby, methyl green, viridian, aquamarine, phenosafranine, incandescent orange, scarlet-fever purple, cyanic blue, tessellated bronze, hospital-fruit-basket orange,…"[15] (fig. 12)

On the Strip and on Vermont Street, the city definitely still glitters, and when seen at night from afar, it seems like a mirage. But its skyline has changed enormously, and crowds now gather on the Strip/Promenade by day to admire the new architectural wonders. The resort hotel-casinos consist of tall constructions which are similar, yet differentiated by specific elements characteristic to their theme: pyramids at the Luxor, the Excalibur castle, the St. Mark's Tower at The Venetian, the Mirage volcano, and fountains at the Bellagio, are now the architectural "signs" denoting the identity of each casino; no longer, or not only, are there neon signs. Within the dimension of architecture of communication (Venturi), there has been a move from a phase of signs to one of narration. Indeed, the new resort hotel-casinos seem to offer what we can call a narrative model of architecture, a three-dimensional narrative, a sort of beautiful fairy-tale that has the power to transport us – as Beth Dunlop writes about Disneyland – "towards other kingdoms," into a world of imagination and dreams.[16]

But what happened to the original signs once destruction of the old motel-casinos changed the face of the Strip? Within the YESCO (Young Electric Sign Company) graveyard – YESCO, property of a Mormon family dating back to the origins of the city, was the most important company in its field – an effort was undertaken for salvage and historical recovery of the signs, which led to the foundation of The Neon Museum. And thus began the phase of treating the old Las Vegas as if it were a museum, creating a repertory of its memory. "Welcome to Fabulous Las Vegas," the famous sign designed by Betty Willis in 1950, continues to shine in the center of the Strip, while the most impressive image perhaps remains the Flamingo Hilton – as previously mentioned. With orange and purple lights in the shape of a shell, it shines in the night like a "beautiful bejeweled woman," to use Howard Hughes' metaphor, recalled by Norman Mailer. However, the two neon palms that were part of the Dunes' Oasis Casino sign, yet another example of Raul Rodriguez's art, were recycled to a literally "exotic" place: a Bangkok nightclub called NASA. The Aladdin, which reopened in 2001 after complete renovation, no longer displays its memorable Aladdin's lamp, and the Stardust has lost its cascade of glittery stardust.

> *"The night before I left Las Vegas I walked out in the desert to look at the moon. There was a jeweled city on the horizon, spires rising in the night, but the jewels were diadems of electric and the spires were the neon of signs ten stories high."*
> *Norman Mailer*

Together with hosts of neon signs, other relics from the old Las Vegas were also, so to speak, put in the attic. While showgirl numbers continue to represent an integral part of the live entertainment, the most famous "girls" are now part of the past, from the "Ziegfeld Follies" who accompanied Frank Sinatra in one of his first shows at the Sands, to the tall, beautiful Lido de Paris dancers who lit up nights at the Stardust until 1991. The best-selling shows today have an entirely different flavor, from the highly refined Cirque du Soleil, on the bill at Treasure Island for years now, to the original Blue Man Group at the Luxor. More recently, *Titanic* singer Celine Dion was chosen as the regular star for at least three years at Caesars' new "Colosseum," a 4,000 seat megatheater. (fig. 13)

In the epilogue to his lengthy essay, Moehring writes, "No one even thirty years ago could have predicted this transformation, but Las Vegas has dramatically reinvented itself, becoming another Parthenon, another Taj Mahal, another spectacle for globetrotting tourists. The city's pioneers could never have envisioned that their sleepy whistlestop in the remote Mohave Desert would someday host this shrine to the glorification of leisure."[17]

> *"This is a fabulous extraordinary madhouse. All around is desert sand with pink and purple mountains on the horizon. All the big hotels are luxe to the last degree… The lighting at night is fantastic."*
> *Noel Coward*

Las Vegas changed radically over the course of just a few decades. From the mecca for gambling and money laundering, the "Sin City" that represented the complementary face to puritan America has attempted, at least in the last decade, to recapture its virginity, so to speak, and to play a new hand, converting itself into a destination, in Disney style, for vacationing families. This operation has been only partially successful: while there is still Circus Circus, the other hotel-casinos are backtracking and shows are going back to an erotic focus. But there is one thing that Las Vegas can't undo – the fact that it has become a unique site of some the most daring and audacious architec-

13. Las Vegas: Caesars Palace, View of Statues, Colosseum Theater, and Planet Hollywood

tural experimentation and adulteration, experimentation in search of a more educated and sophisticated public that doesn't just appreciate the comfort and luxury of the new resorts, but that also appreciates and wants to know the origin of their style and design.

And finally, from an air conditioned nightmare – in the words of Henry Miller – it is becoming a repository for a new idea of culture and art that belongs to a phase successive to postmodernism, which we cannot yet fully define. It is in any case a symbol of a young America, enthusiastic over what's new at all costs, that destroys all traces of history to follow the myth of progress and of ever increasing modernity. In this sense, Las Vegas truly becomes the new global city, the simulacrum of simulacra: a chameleonic city that lives on clichés while simultaneously destroying them, that absorbs and reproduces everything. Through the urban theme, which is the latest trend – at least until now – in the architecture and décor of resort hotel-casinos, the standardized cities of the world are recycled here, becoming an "archive," a concentrate of collective and mass memory: history "encapsulated," as it were, and at the same time a negation of history.

This mix of "new and nostalgia" bears witness to another paradox: on the one hand, Las Vegas seems projected only into the future, and not into the past. On the other, we are already witnessing a revival phenomenon, a return to the origins of Las Vegas through recovery of the 1950s and 1960s. Until just recently, those eras were considered the height of kitsch, but now they have become history. Collections of fetishes and "memorabilia" can be seen in the hotel-casinos, such as the series of murals by artist Steve Kaufman that decorate the inside of Caesars Palace celebrating the *vintage* Caesars. Above all, in the University of Nevada, Las Vegas, Libraries, thanks to various purchases and donations, visitors can go back over the city's recent past, in a memory by now widely shared, and almost feel a sense of regret, a suffused sense of nostalgia stemming from a romantic view of a Las Vegas lost, but also, and this we cannot forget, a violent Las Vegas sometimes of questionable taste. And there are scholars/curious minds who investigate the revival phenomenon: hence the memories of a city, chosen as the model for American pop sensibility, become the object of refined cultural analysis. All of this is done in an effort not to forget, because the present always comes from the past, that is, from our view of the past.

Thus, at the meeting held in 2001 at the University of Nevada, Las Vegas, with the participation of José Gamez, Dave Hickey, and others, and published in the magazine *Architecture Las Vegas* (2001), the choice of subject was no coincidence. This group of design scholars and professionals found itself discussing "What have we made here?," or rather, the past and future of Las Vegas, its theme architecture, and how that can clash with non-theme architecture. In a paradoxical prophecy, they conclude that shortly, to come almost full circle, the theme for the resort of the new millennium could be "Las Vegas–Las Vegas."

Van Gorp- So, what's next? Steve Wynn (former owner of the Bellagio, now wealthy patron of the Wynn Collection) says theming is over. So where are we going next with all of this? Where's the Strip going?

Hickey- I would say that, stylistically, if I were doing something now I would open a retro neon casino.

Gamez- Do a Las Vegas–Las Vegas.

So, now, a copy is just a copy of itself![18]

14. Las Vegas: Bellagio Hotel, Atrium with Flowers/Sculpture by Dale Chihuly, (*credit: Bellagio Hotel)

But, beyond gambling and extravagant architecture, visitors to the "new" Las Vegas will find themselves presented with unprecedented cultural offerings. Several years ago – out of a collaboration between UNLV professor Richard Wiley, Nobel Laureate Wole Soyinka, and Mandalay Resort Group President Glenn Schaeffer – the International Institute of Modern Letters was founded; it participates in the Cities of Asylum program in partnership with the International Parliament of Writers in Paris, offering asylum to talented writers and artists of few means or under persecution in their home countries, who then hold conferences or performances. Casinos, moreover, often hold not just shows but academic conventions. In a sense, there seems to be a return to the educational purpose of the Grand Tour. Is Las Vegas, in its infinite metamorphoses, perhaps becoming an art capital as well? Galleries are springing up, and museums are opening; after the great copy phase there has been a move to originals: the Bellagio paved the way with an art gallery rich with French impressionist paintings, the pride of ingenious businessman Steve Wynn. Now, Wynn has even opened a gallery at his own personal headquarters, the Wynn Collection, where the historic Desert Inn once stood. And his new project, following the sale of the Bellagio to MGM Mirage, is to build a new resort originally called "Le Rêve" from his favorite Picasso painting in his collection, and now named Wynn Las Vegas: no longer an Italian-themed resort, but a "domestic, desert architecture of the West." So, will this be the next trend? It certainly won't be the last.

"An artsy scene with a Vegas twist."[19]

Reflection on change in the city of Las Vegas, and on an overcoming of the concept of the art/architecture defined as postmodern, is thus joined by a change in the role of a museum today. Underlying this reflection is also a rethinking of the concept of culture in today's society. "Las Vegas has more to export than mere gaming. In the transformation to entertainment as the basis of culture, Las Vegas leads all others," as Rothman points out.[20] And Dave Hickey, perhaps the critic most committed in the 1990s to investigating this nexus between art and popular culture through the phenomenology of Las Vegas, collaborated recently with Alex Farquharson and Libby Lumpkin on a very interesting exhibit precisely on the topic of "The Convergence of Art and Las Vegas." The exhibit, entitled "The Magic Hour," was held at the Neue Galerie in Graz.

Today, the Strip presents itself as a system for modern rationalization of "land-use," of the accumulation and combination of forms and styles which are modern/postmodern/and beyond, and finally, as an exuberant unfurling of playful imagination and unbridled experimentation. It is no coincidence that one of the most audacious architects of the post-postmodern, Dutchman Rem Koolhaas, tried to bring new meaning to the idea of architectural space, precisely in Las Vegas and precisely within The Venetian. Vast spaces with a massive, compact cubic structure will host traveling exhibits, whether of a traditional nature or linked to modern design.

Thus, in a joining of high and popular art, one of the most sought after architects of the moment revives the idea of a "global museum" – in line with the cultural policy of Thomas Krens, director of the Solomon R. Guggenheim Foundation – by designing two galleries inside a casino. In a recent interview by

15. Las Vegas: Bellagio Hotel, Conservatory

Alessandro Scotti, Koolhaas sums up as follows his theory of architecture as movement:[21] "Architecture comes to life through its 'erotic' drive to systematically define and fill the space. Remember the expression 'nature hates emptiness'? I'd paraphrase that as 'Architecture hates emptiness.' Maybe that's why I'm interested in the properties and potential of emptiness in terms of organizing an architect's ambitions. The element of 'emptiness' has always held a central position in our projects."

If, on the whole, Las Vegas is dominated by an architecture of excess, of accumulation without empty spaces, the placing of two museums in The Venetian creates a shock effect that leads to dialectic reflection on the full/empty relationship in architecture and urban planning. And Koolhaas, who has not forgotten his training as a scriptwriter, states: "I think the art of a scriptwriter is to conceive sequences of episodes which build suspense and a chain of events…The largest part of my work is montage – spatial montage."[22]

The walls of the Guggenheim Hermitage Museum are wrapped in steel panels wrought with a special technique designed to give them the look of a soft, burnished classical velvet. At this time (that is, during the writing of this text), the museum hosts a rich collection of twentieth-century impressionist and avant-garde painters from the Hermitage in St. Petersburg. The other museum, the Guggenheim Las Vegas, uses shiny metal to cover high walls in a square, hangar-like space with a glass ceiling to let in light (a sort of cyberspace perhaps close to the tastes of The Venetian owner, millionaire Sheldon Adelson, who made a fortune in electronics and periodically organizes the sizable COMDEX convention); the effect is much less jarring and unexpected in respect to the frescoed halls hosting copies of the Venetian masters. Its first event has been an exhibit designed for the Guggenheim New York by the other star of American architecture today, Frank O. Gehry, who gained universal fame for the Guggenheim Bilbao and who inaugurated, in October 2003, with a great display of publicity and fireworks, the Walt Disney Concert Hall in Los Angeles.

An enormous change has occurred in recent years in the museum system, in which the container now seems more important than the contents: you go to see the museums by Koolhaas, Botta, Meier, or Gehry, even before the works exhibited within those buildings. But if this is the case in big cities with a tradition in art, what effect will it have in Las Vegas? In regard to what are now familiarly called the "Googs," Scott Dickensheets asks: "What are museums – particularly in the context of the Las Vegas Strip?" Will they blend into the design that has by now turned Las Vegas into an icon, or will they clash with the context forever? An initial response may come from Robert Tracy, art historian at UNLV. According to Tracy, not only will the new museums not fail, but precisely for their "difference," they will give new impetus to the life of museums as places for audacious and risky artistic planning instead of as stagnant mortuaries. "There will be those who say the museums are nothing more than upscale casino greeters. But history will prove these skeptics wrong."[23] While we don't want to pass judgment on such a delicate issue, it cannot be denied that people today are talking about art also in Las Vegas, and what's more, they're making it. The Guggenheim Heritage Museum remains active, but the Guggenheim Las Vegas closed in 2003 for good, while the Bellagio gallery has put its collection of impressionist art on the auction block. Nevertheless, Las Vegas's contribution to the discourse surrounding museums and culture will remain important.

"All the hotels are on the same pattern. A gambling casino with angular shafts of light falling on to the gamblers; the perpetual noise of the slot machines and the cries of the crap shooters; a bar lounge with a separate four- or five-piece band playing continually."

Noel Coward, Nescafé Society

In a U.S. panorama that generally lacks old buildings and artistic tradition, hotels (like 1930s movie theaters) have often represented a place of luxury and exclusiveness, sometimes even becoming monuments of imposing architecture and grandiose interiors, historical landmarks to preserve, microcosms to study. Above all, we think of the hotels built between the late 1800s and the 1930s, some of which still twinkle with numerous stars. The United States has also led in construction of another sort of urban landscape: that of anonymous motels, often only one storey high, sporting a typical neon sign. U.S. highways are (or better were) studded with them, as were cities like Los Angeles until just recently. Even Las Vegas – as we have seen – went through a motel-casino phase in the 1950s.

"Hotels for the 21st Century: Hotels as art galleries."

Recently, however, the situation has changed in Las Vegas and elsewhere. Enterprising business men and audacious designers have changed the idea of the hotel: from New York to Los Angeles to Miami, the Ian Schrager–Philippe Starck duo have turned the hotel into a place no longer just for sleeping or passing through; it has become a new residence and more importantly a place to visit in and for itself, "a place to be seen." Hotel bars and restaurants are decorated with works of art, and interior décor has become a trendy discipline halfway between minimalist rigor and the appeal of fusion. Bold combinations of antique, ethnic, and ultramodern pieces decorate atriums and halls, which thus become the stage for theatrical or cinematic installations, winter gardens, fashion catwalks.

Las Vegas, which has itself become an enormous design lab, has done no less, meeting the needs of a new, more sophisticated and wealthy clientele. However, the difference with Las Vegas lies in excess, and its search for the beautiful and the new is, in any case, always linked to the entertainment principle, which has now – in the words of David E. Brown – become *pancultural fun*: "Vegas is known for its fantasy, for suspending time in reality, for transfixing the guest all over the world. It's Vegas, but it also wants to be the world. Las Vegas is not about intimacy and discretion. It is bold and playful."[24]

Two examples, which we will come back to in the last chapter of this book, speak for all: first, the *postindustrial chic*[25] of the Bellagio, with its atrium decorated by over 2,000 gigantic, colored glass flowers entitled "Flowers of Como," by sculptor Dale Chihuly (fig. 14); its *conservatory* always with fresh flowers recalling aristocratic villas in Italy and England (fig. 15); its Gallery of Fine Art and the exclusive Picasso restaurant that hosts an incredible collection of original drawings by the great Spanish painter. Second, The Venetian, where the spirit of Renaissance and Baroque Venice (figs. 16,17) is "inimitably" translated into a new vocabulary of arches, balustrades, bridges, and frescoed ceilings in a pure mix-and-match style.[26] Both are hotels designed for a clientele that wants luxury, comfort, and fun guaranteed. (figs. 18-21)

16. Las Vegas: The Venetian Hotel, Galleria Frescoes

17. Las Vegas: The Venetian Hotel, Doge's Palace Columns, Detail

18. *Las Vegas: The Venetian Hotel,*
Doge's Palace, Detail

19. *Las Vegas: The Venetian Hotel,*
Doge's Palace, Detail

20. *Las Vegas: The Venetian Hotel,*
Doge's Palace, Detail

21. *Las Vegas: The Venetian Hotel,*
Doge's Palace, Detail

"Las Vegas (What?) Las Vegas (Can't hear you! Too noisy) Las Vegas!!!"
Tom Wolfe

In conclusion, the question is whether Las Vegas has its own style, if it is indeed still possible to speak of "style" today. And what relation does the "Vegas" of the Strip (meaning the one described by Venturi in the 1970s) have with the "new" Las Vegas and with that other city that has spread out between the desert and the hills, Summerlin or Green Valley? Just as Vegas style can be identified with the adulteration and overcoming of styles, in a "diversity of images" of which even Moehring speaks,[27] in the same way, the entire city of Las Vegas is not just a "city," but a conglomerate of cities strapped in by a belt. (figs. 22,23)

And its style: is it a simple return to eclecticism with references ranging from classic to vernacular? A sort of neobaroque, to quote Italian semiotician Omar Calabrese? Or still something else? Perhaps the idea of style cannot be applied to Las Vegas: Robert Venturi[28] sees the city as an example of "our multiple taste cultures," while José Gamez confirms that there are many styles in architecture, and that in the case of Las Vegas, it is better to speak of "experience." In revisiting the Grand Tour, in the next chapter, it could be said, in the words of Wayne Curtis, that "the experience of place has been replaced by the place of experience."[29]

22. *Las Vegas: The Venetian Hotel, Contarini-Fasan Palace, Detail*

23. *Las Vegas: The Venetian Hotel, Marciana Library, Detail*

3. The Grand Tour in Italy Revisited

"O, Ma, dear! O, Papa! Do look! Isn't this charming! Isn't it delightful!"
On the Grand Tour, Punch, or The London Charivari, *Oct. 10, 1876*

The syndrome of mass tourism is not a phenomenon exclusive to our times. Lord Byron built a romantic image of himself as a wanderer, contributing to the diffusion of the Orientalist myth in the early 1800s. He was already aware that the sense of *déjà-vu* evoked by actual landscapes, seen "live," cannot be disregarded. Like many of his fellow countrymen, the poet couldn't resist the desire for a completely literary and slightly mannered exoticism, one that for more than a century had become a fashionable phenomenon, moving like a restless pilgrim in search of a lost Eden, in Greece or Italy.

As Byron wrote in *Don Juan* (V, 52), brushing aside superficial and hurried travelers with a sarcastic sneer:

Every fool describes, in these bright days,
His wondrous journey to some foreign court,
And spawns his quarto, and demands your praise
   […]
While Nature, tortured twenty thousand ways,
Resigns herself, with exemplary patience,
To guide-books, rhymes, tours, sketches, illustrations.

This construction of an imaginary of travel to far-off, exotic lands also includes the Grand Tour adventure, which out of their profound desire to escape, leads travelers to seek out new, extreme sensations in unknown places, if not in "other" worlds. In addition to escape, the motivations behind such travel are many: a thirst for knowledge and conquest, a need for new horizons, the recovery of health, a more intense life. Indeed, what is seen is often less important than the meaning uncovered by the traveler's gaze.

This, however, is no recent discovery. Around the beginning of the second century A.D., Pliny the Younger wrote: "We travel by land and sea, to see things we wouldn't even glance at if they were right before our eyes. This happens because that's how nature made things: we prefer what is far-off and remain indifferent to what is close by, whether because desire loses intensity when easy to satisfy, or because we become disinterested in things we can see whenever we like, convinced that we will soon have another chance to pass by them."

If there is something that does change through the centuries, it is the means of travel, along with a different perception of space and time. The romantic traveler *à la* Byron went slowly and with difficulty, moving progressively closer to the desti-

24. Rome: Roman Forum

nations on his itinerary as if on pilgrimage. It was a hard conquest that entailed negotiation with what was left behind and with a new landscape and all its historical and artistic layers. Experience of a place could not be translated simply as rational knowledge; it touched the most profound emotional sphere. Such experiences were true encounters, (as defined by Stephen Greenblatt in *Marvellous Possessions*), which would become writing experiences. In times closer to ours, the notebooks of Bruce Chatwin, anomalous traveler to Patagonia, Afghanistan, and the Australian desert, bear witness to this once again.

As of today, there is virtually no unexplored place on earth capable of inspiring similar adventures of discovery. Distances have been reduced to almost nothing by airplane flights and difficulties minimized by easy, comfortable travel – or at least that's what we all thought until September 11, 2001; at the same time, television and Internet communication give the impression that we are experiencing events from all over the world, live and nonstop. Everything seems familiar and partakes of standardization, as we used to say, or of globalization, as we now say. This makes many cities seem like copies of one another. You can find the same products, the same gadgets, in any mall, in any big city, anywhere in the Western world, or at least in the more industrially advanced world. Most inner cities experience the same dangers and encounter the same problems.

Yet we are also experiencing a curious paradox. If everything said so far is true for most of the world, from the U.S. to Japan, new differences have arisen that have nothing to do with tourist travel or with a general allure of the exotic. And, if we have the eyes to see them, these differences confront us with dramatic realities. How, for example, can we fully enjoy the startling beauty of the temples and

25. Rome: Colosseum (72/80 A.D.)

palaces of the maharajahs in India without feeling a pang of sadness at the sight of thousands of poor, hungry people who can by no means be considered as picturesque furniture! And how can we experience the wilderness parks in Africa when environmental destruction and the diffusion of horrible diseases, such as AIDS, are with us! The multicultural society many dreamed of now seems a utopia that is becoming a universal dystopia. Travel as a means of getting to know and appreciate the *other* with all its differences seems increasingly more difficult. Only one of two possibilities can hold true: either the other has already become like us, or the other is not open to being known. Knowledge of the other, of the place that is visited, must also become knowledge of ourselves, so we can come back from the experience changed. Often, this meeting/clash between knowledge of the other

26. Rome: Arch of Constantine (315 A.D.)

27. Rome: Arch of Septimius Severus (203 A.D), Detail

and revelation of self can be quite a shock. A good example of this is the experience of the protagonist in *The Sheltering Sky* by Paul Bowles, or E. M. Forster's suggestions in *A Passage to India*. The encounter with an outside and distant world, such as Morocco or India in the two examples cited here, with traditions that are often incomprehensible to the Western observer, can be an upsetting, and even painful, experience.

"Mais les vrais voyageurs sont ceux-là qui partent pour partir...."
Charles Baudelaire

All this is part of the consciousness of modernity, whose condition is incessant travel and whose spirit is doubt. The same is true for the literature that documents it; as Susan Sontag has stressed on numerous occasions, "modern travel writing is a literature of disappointment." Similarly – as a strategy for eluding that "sense of failure" – the renowned anthropologist Claude Lévi-Strauss suggests that we look at the world, clearly already discovered and familiar to us, with new eyes. He himself plays with disguise, knowing full well that "real travel" belongs to others, from the past. What is lost forever to the modern traveler is the "marvelous spectacle" of full vision, a reality once attainable but now gone. As Mark Twain had already perceived in *Innocents Abroad*, in Rome we can no longer claim to have been "the first."[30] So, is the Grand Tour now just a myth that smacks of *d'antan*?

In the 1800s, priest and university professor Antonio Stoppani wrote a book on the romantic idea of an Italy consisting of natural and cultural landscapes, cities of art and picturesque places. He called his book *Il bel paese* (*The Beautiful Country*), leaving the expression as a legacy for generations to come.

The Grand Tour was a cosmopolitan phenomenon. Travelers were not just English or European (Americans comprised a large number in the 1800s), and Italy was not the only destination, though a trip to Italy was a mandatory stop, a rite of passage so to speak. Indeed, its monuments and landscapes were a favorite subject in painting starting in the 1600s. One need hardly mention Goethe and Byron, John Singer Sargent, Henry James, Horace Walpole, and Elizabeth Barrett Browning. In regard to the last, her Italian experience was both intellectual and personal, not to speak of her dog Flush, who later became the main character of a lovely book by Virginia Woolf.

Even at the time of the "vintage" Grand Tour, successive stages and phases were already visible. Take, for example, the words of Doctor Johnson who wrote "A man who has not been to Italy will be forever aware of his inferiority for not having seen what a man should see"; and those of Horace Walpole who wrote to his poet friend Thomas Gray from Rome: "Come see Rome and Italy before the Italians destroy it." It is no coincidence that we have mentioned Walpole's name twice, because it is precisely to him we owe the first "gothic" novel to English literature, *The Castle of Otranto* (1764). The work is full of fantastic and supernatural stories set in imaginary medieval times, dictated by the same taste for gothic medievalism that led him to build the architectural oddity of his mini-castle Strawberry Hill.

Two opposing types of comments can be found coming from the United States in relation to what Van Vyck Brooks defines as the "Arcadian dream": the beautiful Italy cherished by Henry James, Nathaniel Hawthorne's "site of romance"; or on the contrary, the anti-Grand Tour portrayed ironically by Mark Twain and depicting a dirty and decaying, ignorant and superstitious Italy.

> *"Next to the Colosseum there are perhaps the most stupendous of all Roman remains. All travellers to Rome will have been familiar with the prints of Piranesi, which made popular and, as it were, anthologized the ruins of Rome.…This is, indeed, a surviving feature from the Grand Tour."*
> *Sacheverell Sitwell,* Grand Tour: A Journey in the Tracks of Aristocracy, *1937*
> (figs. 24,25)

> *"The arch of Constantine, and the Coliseum, which frowned on me in black masses through the soft but deepening twilight…gave me the most bewildering idea of the grandeur and extent of ancient Rome."*
> *Anna Jameson,* Diary of an Ennuyée, *1834 (figs. 26,27)*

Reality, imagination, and cliché become essential components for both the experience and the narrative of the Grand Tour. European and American visitors seem to be mostly (if not exclusively) interested in the Italy of the past: a country reduced to a single dimension, a mixture of beauty and ruins, of shattered glory and of decadence, magnificence, and corruption all at once. Such a Grand Tour seems immediately to belong to the past, forever born from realities and (more often) stereotypes that, over time, will cause its nature to change to tourism, and today into mass tourism.

> An English newspaper reads: "Venice, Florence and Rome – 9 nights from only £799 – Three of Italy's most magical and glorious cities are combined in this superb Page & Moy holiday. Romantic Venice, with its myriad canals and waterways; beautiful Florence, birthplace of the Renaissance, and Rome – the Eternal City."

If modern technologies have radically upset the travel experience, in any case there remains "an internal predisposition to confronting diversity, a desire to experiment unknown realities capable of widening personal knowledge horizons. And hence travel becomes an increasingly mental operation, an attitude toward confrontation that presupposes openness to what is unusual, unknown, or a surprise, and above all to more detached reflection on one's own starting place."[31] Or, again, a new perspective that brings profound meaning back to travel is the simultaneously fascinating and upsetting discovery of something new and different, under the guise of something familiar and obvious or even banal.

Thus, travel is not always synonymous with actual movement. The term "mobility" means "the quality or condition of being mobile" (*Oxford Dictionary*); it presumes a space or place in which movement, represented in most cases by travel, occurs. As Leslie Fiedler observed in *The Return of the Vanishing American*,[32] American geography has a mythological property, and from its colonial foundations American writers have tended to define their country in topological terms. The space, the land, "an immensity of populated colors," as Elio Vittorini wrote, "is thus the America we speak of."

28. Rome: Arch of Titus (81 A.D.)

Mobility is therefore a constitutive element of America as a nation, a way of looking for its own identity through continuous progress and change. Mobility is seen as a mental attitude and as real movement, where movement is a tendency toward frontiers, toward conquest, expatriation, or exile, from inside to outside its own borders and shores. Yet it is also mobility as a synonym for perpetual change, renewal, the myth of eternal youth: what is always "new," both as ideology and as a model.

It is no coincidence that cinema, the first example of art in movement, is typically American, despite the fact that it was born in Europe. Jean Baudrillard writes that American culture is space, speed, cinema, and technology, "together with the flow and mobility of the screen." Many are the stereotypes, followed in part also by Baudrillard in his highly debated essay *Amérique*,[33] that reiterate opposition between the Old World, or a static Europe grown up over the ruins of History, and the New World – a "Brave New World"– where continuous territorial re-mapping prevails over the dimension of time and history, though nevertheless stereotypes and sometimes prejudices, imitation of the old and modelization of the new, still frequently coexist.

29. Las Vegas: Caesars Palace, Entrance Archway

Think of Umberto Eco's writings on the "periphery of the empire," or the post-modern condition of which Jean-François Lyotard speaks in a famous essay. In all these cases, there is constant movement across the ocean, of persons and ideas, fashions and styles, in an exchange that raises the question: who is imitating who? And finally, today, in the era of globalization, Las Vegas presents a model for a city as laboratory of the future: rather than dream or reality, "it is a hyperreality, like a utopia lived from the beginning as if it had been realized."[34] It is "hysterical movement in-place" (F. S. Fitzgerald) or "hysterical land" (Baudrillard) as the flourishing and uninterrupted movement of fashion, meaning a vibration within immobilism.

But is traveling always movement? And how should we consider traveling on the Internet? You can travel within your own room, in the style of Montaigne and Pascal; or take the English travels of Des Esseintes's decadent hero, which consisted of a mental journey because reality could never give him the same pleasure as his imagination. You can take refuge in your imagination and travel like Emilio Salgari (1863–1911), the Italian author of so many popular adventure novels who traveled over the seas of Malaysia, Papua New Guinea, and the Sunda Islands without ever leaving Turin; he had boundless paper archives behind him, filled with travel books and geographical maps. Or you can visit Stevenson's *Treasure Island*. Robert Louis Stevenson really did travel, but as a true "Tusitala"

30. Las Vegas: Bellagio Hotel, Detail

(Teller of the Tales, as the Samoan natives called him), he invented the island on paper, a product of his wild imagination for the enjoyment of his son, as well as that of generations of readers to come. "I travel for travel's sake," wrote Stevenson, "And then to write about it, if the public will be so indulgent as to read my work."

But does it make any difference to us, navigators of the imagination, to read the description of landing on an island in Stevenson's accounts from *In the South Seas*, or to instead read about the landing of the "Italian Robinsons," as penned by Salgari? In both cases, "the world was mobile and plastic: adventure was still possible: though already defeated, pirates could still take to the seas. Treasures existed, and men had not yet repressed the rich and whimsical imaginations of childhood and adolescence," wrote Pietro Citati.[35] At most we could say, like Salgari's shipwreck victims, "Is that our island, or another one?"[36]

Or perhaps, in our era devoid of illusions, there remains an ironic game of citations and pastiche typical of postmodern "rewriting." While a crude reality has taken the object of our desire from us, nothing can stop us from recreating it – novice yet disenchanted, "belated romantics" – in our imagination. There are no limits to adventures on paper!

> *"The 'via sacra' of that dream led through the desert to Las Vegas."*
> *Nick Tosches*[37]
> (figs. 28,29)

And, lastly, we have virtual travel, vicarious travel in place, what America created with its "theme parks" in the era of Walt Disney. This topic was the subject of a highly interesting essay entitled *The Theming of America*, in which author Mark Gottdiener analyzes the symbolism of a "themed environment" in various American cities, including Las Vegas. "Las Vegas, once a mecca for alcohol, sex, and gambling, has become the theme park capital of the United States as casinos switch to family oriented entertainment and spectacular fantasy façades, such as the Luxor Hotel with its ancient Egypt motif."[38] And it is precisely in Las Vegas that theme architecture finds its apotheosis. Indeed, in Las Vegas you can visit the most distant lands – Egypt and Rome, Paris or the Italian lakes, New York or the Malaysian jungle – without ever leaving the Nevada desert. The imagination replaces real movement with virtual travel: a voyage that realizes itself around an autonomous, self-referential universe which is the new resort hotel-casino. (figs. 30,31)

As in nineteenth-century London, when the entire world was brought forth and exhibited in gigantic "cineramas," the same seems to be occurring today in Las Vegas through skillful rebuilding of traditional Grand Tour destinations. The same transformation of typical sites in the theme park tradition also occurred with the great Expositions, between the end of the 1800s and the 1930s. At that time, architects' imaginations blended the legacy of the past with the utopia of the future. Sumptuous pavilions dedicated to the various countries around the world were thus exhibited in a cinematic fashion, in "these gigantic pedestrian-oriented carnivals of industrialism," which ran along the sidewalks inside the Malls.[39]

> *"Nothing is simple in Venice, because it is not a city. It is an archipelago."*
> *Jean Paul Sartre*

Rome, Florence, Como, the Hill Towns in Umbria and Tuscany, and above all Venice evoke magical, "dreamlike" scenarios. Venice is the epitome of the Grand Tour, forever old yet forever new, decadent yet reborn in the experiences of those who are truly capable of seeing her. A city for the eyes, writes Mary McCarthy, built on the water, a never-ending succession of reflections and echoes, a mirror game, a *trompe l'oeil*, because every word uttered is the echo of another, since ancient times. With rare foresight, in *Italian Hours* Henry James wrote that "Venice has been painted and described many thousands of times, and of all the cities of the world is the easiest to visit without going there."[40]

(figs. 32,33)

"If one wanted to travel overnight in somewhere incomparable, to a fantastic mutation of normal reality, where would one go? To Venice, of course."
Thomas Mann

Thus, within the phenomenology of travel, we now find ourselves facing another paradox: that it is possible to "visit" a city without going there. But is this limited to Venice, or is it a paradigm of what travel will be in the future? Following Venturi, Scott Brown, and Izenour, must we continue "Learning from Las Vegas"? In this sense, Las Vegas becomes the symbol of America and of the new global city. If differences seem to be disappearing everywhere, in Las Vegas those differences are rebuilt and reinvented through the "Urban motif," in the latest trend in architectural design and décor, based precisely on the stereotypes. And, the Grand Tour which was supposed to accompany the traveler into adulthood, now seems to lead back to a sort of perennial childhood, to a Wonderland or Never-Never Land where – like newfound Peter Pans – life is lived by these "grown-ups" in a dimension devoted to entertainment and fun. However, there is sometimes the suspicion that the game is not joyful liberty, but rather a sort of "forced play," as Ermanno Bencivenga suggests when he denounces the "society of fun."[41]

31. Bellagio, Lake Como: Grand Hotel Villa Serbelloni, (1852), Detail

32. Venice, at Sunset

33. Las Vegas: The Venetian Hotel, Overall View

4. Theoretical Digressions: the Beautiful, the Ugly... the Fake

"When I was young, a sure way to distinguish great architects was through the consistency and originality of their work…This should no longer be the case. Where the Modern masters' strength lay in consistency, ours should lie in diversity."

Robert Venturi

From Romanticism onward, modernity has been characterized by a drive for *unicum*, the original and authentic, at the moment in which the drama of its loss is experienced. Even American culture, especially during the passage from the nineteenth to the twentieth century, felt a constant tension between imitation and originality, and the challenge of modernism can be seen – as Miles Orvell suggests – as the "culture of authenticity." Toward the second half of the twentieth century, we instead faced the "culture of the copy," a more conscious operation than ever with the so-called postmodern. In a fascinating book bearing that very title,[42] Hillel Schwartz states that the copy generally tries to give an idea of the original, and that this occurs in a variety of ways and in numerous fields of cultural production, from literature, to painting, to architecture. Then she points out, with an evident pun, that "the history of art is the history of 'copy rites,' of transformations that take place during acts of copying," where the copies can be both voluntary and involuntary. Almansi and Fink dedicated an anthology to the fake in literature, highlighting that the operations of falsification, parody, and plagiarism bring a text to life, saving it from death. Indeed, often there are good copies and bad originals, not just the opposite. Hence a copy cannot only be considered negative; "by imitation only variety or even originality of invention is produced," wrote Joshua Reynolds in 1774.

Naturally, what is important in defining a copy as false, facsimile, replica, counterfeit, plagiarism, *à la manière de*, and so on, is the author's intention. However, as Umberto Eco stresses, the hard part consists above all in defining the original or authentic. From this perspective, Las Vegas is an ideal place – metaphorically and in actuality – a true laboratory on the idea of the copy and more.

"Are there any originals left or is everything an original? Or is everything a copy?"
Hillel Schwartz

Hal Rothman reveals that the change in attitude toward Las Vegas as a simulacrum of the authentic occurred after the turning point of postmodernism: "In the 1960s and 1970s, with its back-to-the-roots ethos and ongoing search for authentic, such an argument resonated. In a later age, when people clearly understood the difference between authenticity and inauthenticity, but no longer accepted the cultural framing that made conventional authenticity better, Las Vegas made perfect sense."[43]

What is the difference between plagiarism and copy, between fake and forgery? In both cases there is a desire for originality-through-repetition, for revelation-through-simulation. In both cases there is a copying action plus a personal addition, a deviation. But a "fake" is generally a reworking, a creative imitation or emulation, a virtuosic and combinatorial game, amused re-use and conscious retrieval from the warehouses of tradition. (figs. 34,35) A "copy" is a passive remake, lacking in fancy: the greatest falsification lies in believing in a return to the origins, in the recovery of the original. A fake reconstructs the dimension of a work as a game. A fake can be fun, and in its continual deviation from the imaginary, it can in turn produce a new chain of fakes, each with small differences; a mere copy simply produces nostalgia for the model. The Strip exhibits such a wealth of architectural symbolism and allusions, Venturi et al. point out perceptively, which demonstrates that not just ordinary people, but also architects, find pleasure in an architecture that reminds them of something else, perhaps of the East or the Wild West.

"Allusion and comment, on the past or present or on our great commonplaces or old clichés, and inclusion of every-day in the environment, sacred and profane – these are what are lacking in present-day Modern architecture. We can learn about them from Las Vegas as have other artists from their own profane and stylistic sources."[44] Oscar Wilde, the "artist as liar," wrote that "censoring an artist for forgery means confusing an ethical problem with an aesthetic one"; and again, "the one duty we owe to history is to rewrite it." Another writer on fakes and fakers, Umberto Eco, sets the limit between the truth and falsity of a story, in the playing of "make believe," at the level of the novelistic effect in which "you pretend to say true things, but mustn't actually say you're pretending."[45]

"Cities, like dreams, are made of desires and fears."
Italo Calvino

There are many ways to visit Las Vegas. There are those who go without seeing it. There are those who don't want to see it at all. "Only snobs look down on Las Vegas these days," writes Hal Rothman.[46] It's too easy to wrinkle your nose, to speak ironically about Las Vegas and fill pages and pages with what are now banal, even if brilliantly written, observations on the "city of nothing," Zeropolis, as Bruce Bégout recently did with European detachment. We don't mean to say it's not true that Las Vegas "is the superpower of entertainment that dictates the meaning of existence," that "its theme architecture, in a marriage of commercial seduction and infantile imaginary, leads citizens to a blissful dependence on an opium of spectacle and media";[47] one could continue at length in this tone. But if "Las Vegas is simply our urban horizon," as Bégout remarks again, it is so in many ways, which are not always or only negative. It therefore merits our most serious consideration in order to learn from both its negative and positive sides. It is also a place in which to analyze the evolution of the urban space in the postmodern (and the post-post-modern) period, with a different concept of the city in mind: the city-street, with the Strip taking the place of the walkway, and the mall-square-market, with its fake, yet so well imitated, skies! This is how the logic of the market meets an aspiration toward city as meeting place, which in the Old World gathered around a square, or as keeper of a life that moves at a more human rhythm in respect to machine society, and that watches people walk down the sidewalks.[48]

It is also the city of perpetual change and freedom, of renewal and creativity, the last "Frontier Town," as Rothman defines it;[49] while Mauro Calamandrei writes that "Las Vegas has never been afraid of going against the flow and reinventing itself."[50] Architecture scholar Alan Hess claims that Las Vegas has offered an important contribution to the modern Urban Village; while Bellagio Hotel architect Jon Jerde notes: "We are on the threshold of a new epoch in city making. Although architecture, by definition, has always been the world of the built, of the solid, the next big step will be to explore the architecture of change."[51]

According to Sarah Chaplin and Eric Holding, we are witnessing the "posturban" phase, characterized by a stratification of various styles and different eras, by the contradiction-element and the surprise-effect, and above all by the deliberate use of unplanning. This doesn't mean it's all "inauthenticity"; it is rather a "new authenticity," the same authenticity which Rem Koolhaas considers part of an interactive cycle of intertextual references between the city and its own image, between what we shall call traditional reality and virtual reality.[52]

In the play between imitation and innovation, the fundamental idea is that of the copy or fake. Obviously, there are various phases of the fake. The phase of the 1950s and early 1960s, for example, considered as the ultimate symbol of kitsch until just recently, has now entered into history; its documents are exhibited at the University of Nevada, Las Vegas, Libraries for our analysis and nostalgia. What fascinates scholars of the postmodern and beyond in Las Vegas is its presumption of

34. Venice: Doge's Palace (14th/15th Century), Detail, Adam and Eve Sculptures

35. Las Vegas: The Venetian Hotel, Doge's Palace, Detail, Adam and Eve Sculptures (copy)

36. Paolo Caliari, known as Veronese, "Apotheosis of Venice", Grand Council Chamber, Doge's Palace, Venice, Italy (1575/78) (*credit: Musei Civici, Venezia)

37. Las Vegas: The Venetian Hotel, "Apotheosis of Venice" (copy)

"faithfulness" and "difference" at the same time. For example, the canals of The Venetian are traveled by "real gondoliers," but without the rotten smell that sometimes disturbs (or completes) the real Venice; and the frescoes and canvases by Tiepolo and Veronese, often hard to see in dark Venice churches or on the high ceilings in Palazzo Ducale, are well lit, visible, and brand new! (figs. 36,37)

This sensation of estrangement recalls Mark Twain's ironic comment about "innocents abroad"; when examining Leonardo's deteriorated *Last Supper* in Milan, or at the sight of dirty and stinking Venice, he provocatively exclaims, "the copy's a lot better than the original!" It is the same type of estrangement that shows the "real" Venice as if it were "fake" in episodes of the soap opera *The Bold and the Beautiful* shot on location there. On the other hand, haven't you ever had the impression that Venice also has unfortunately turned a bit into Las Vegas?[53]

Discussion recalling Walter Benjamin on the loss of an "aura" is dated with the postmodern. According to José Gamez, concepts of authenticity and the authentic seem out of date in an age marked by the global market and its impact on urban spaces. Where Benjamin suggested a sort of nostalgia for a lost original, complaining at the same time of a cleft in the modern between author and artwork, this was also a sign of the modern impulse to break with tradition in order to find a new language: the avant-garde and whatever else follows.

In truth, this issue is more intricate for architecture, due both to the specificity of the artistic genre and to the long tradition of emulation and imitation ("copy"?) in the period dominated by the Beaux Arts and eclecticism. In this sense, it would seem, paradoxically, that copying is the main way of making architecture. And this is as true as ever in the case of Las Vegas, or at least it seems so. Indeed, once again according to Gamez, traditional criteria for urban architecture are fairly ineffective here, and we must ask what the difference is between a pretense that tends to deceive (the copy or forgery), and one that – through conscious tempting and allusion – tends to distract, seduce, and entertain. Hence the discourse is more complex than it first seems, and it leads to reflection on a new idea of city and on the changed concept of architecture. What is the relationship between a Renaissance city, meant as an ideal and eternal model with buildings that must last over the centuries, and a city like Las Vegas where change is constant and the architecture as ephemeral as the world it comes to represent? If the rule here can be summed up as a revisiting of the 1968 slogan "imagination in power," it is because of the puzzle-type composition that characterizes Las Vegas: a "collage-city"[54] where the pieces are continually taken apart and replaced. It is an as yet unsurpassed example of "Archi-tainment," suggest Gottdiener, Collins, and Dickens[55] with a happy neologism. (figs. 38-41)

Here we will analyze the categories of fake and original, using several transformations/replicas of the St. Mark's Campanile in Venice as a model, starting with the original bell tower and then moving to its ruins after its sudden collapse in 1902. Let's consider the numerous "copies" that have arisen in various places in the United States, and in particular the emblematic example of the Daniels and Fisher Tower in Denver, miraculous survivor of the 1960s demolitions that paved the way for the new Denver with its skyscrapers in concrete and glass. Built between 1909 and 1911 by architect Frederick Junius Sterner, the D&F Tower was supposed to become the symbol of the city. After a visit to Venice, sponsor William C. Daniels

38. Giovanni Antonio Canal, known as Canaletto, "St. Mark's Square", Thyssen-Bornemisza Collection, Madrid, Spain (1724/25)
(*credit Thyssen-Bornemisza Collection)

39. Denver, Colo.: Daniels and Fisher Tower, (1909/11), architect F. J. Sterner

40. Venice: St. Mark's Campanile Tower

41. Las Vegas: The Venetian Hotel, Campanile Tower

65

decided to enhance downtown Denver with a "replica" of the St. Mark's bell tower. Reconstruction of the original bell tower ("dov'era e com'era," as the Venetians said) coincided almost exactly with construction of the new tower in Denver, leading the *Denver Times* to write: "Venetians are erecting a column [that is an] almost exact replica of the D&F Tower in Denver."[56]

That comment can be considered much more than a paradoxical remark. In this regard, we would like to briefly mention the case of the ship of Theseus, which through numerous re-readings and interpretations has become a logic puzzle as "identity paradox." Plutarch (*Lives*, Theseus 23, 1) says that the ship of Theseus underwent continual replacement of its parts over the course of its travels, until at a certain point, it no longer contained any of the original parts. Later, in *De Corpore* (XI, 7), Hobbes invites readers to suppose that someone secretly kept all the old parts of the ship in order to build another ship identical to the original. That ship, named *Argo,* is also used by Roland Barthes as allegory for the object that depends on two acts, substitution and nomination, an object "with no other cause but its name, with no other identity but its shape."[57]

So now the question is: which of the two ships is "authentic"? The first, which has kept its name and continuity of function, or the second which consists of the material substance? And, in the case of the series of copies of the St. Mark's bell tower, what role is played by the last of the copies in terms of time, which now stands in front of The Venetian in Las Vegas?

Once into the copy mechanism, the series could be infinite. However, no example is a true "copy" because, when searching for the "as if" effect, everything seems "other." And if there is an undeniable pleasure in seeing an authentic work of art, there can also be incomparable pleasure in seeing the copy, the fake. As Umberto Eco once wrote of Disneyland in an Aristotelian aside, something we can also apply to Las Vegas: "The pleasure of imitation, as the ancients knew, is one of the most innate in the human spirit. But here we not only enjoy a perfect imitation, we also enjoy the conviction that imitation has reached its apex and afterwards reality will always be inferior to it."[58]

And finally, couldn't we say that the originality of Las Vegas – pardon the joke – consists of its being an ensemble of copies, and what's more, of copies of copies? On the other hand, as Omar Calabrese wrote in regard to what he calls the "cocktail effect" in music, just as in architecture and fashion, "in contemporary times, which abound with desire for continual innovation, radical innovation is paradoxically impossible, and one almost always ends up citing something already written or seen. So just imagine the surprise one feels upon seeing the birth of something new, not from an involuntary repetition, but from an intentional program referring to something culturally stable. The appearance of something new from what is programmatically old consists almost of a miracle."[59] There are hosts of examples. Here, we will only mention one detail in the great Caesars Palace complex, where the pool entitled Neptune's Bath (fig. 42) resembles another pool of the same name, in that other monument to the fake, the Hearst Castle in San Simeon, more closely than it does the Roman baths. In the great civil and religious architecture of the United States between the nineteenth and twentieth centuries, imitations of Classical, Gothic, and Roman styles showed almost rigorous adherence to their models. Quite differently, in Las Vegas – with few exceptions – there is no respect for the original or its context, but only for imagination and excess, in a word, for fun.

"Bad taste suffers the same fate that Croce recognized as typical of art: everyone knows full well what it is, and no one fears identifying or preaching about it, but there's a bit of embarrassment over defining it."

Umberto Eco

What is beautiful and what is ugly in Las Vegas? We agree with Remo Ceserani[60] that the category of *kitsch* must be reviewed, not just in general, but also in the specific case of Las Vegas. The *camp* phase is also over in part, though it brought a clear change in taste in the 1960s, just preceding the "revolution" of postmodern and pop art. As Susan Sontag's writings reveal: "Camp taste turns its back on the good-bad axis of ordinary aesthetic judgement. Camp doesn't reverse things. It doesn't argue that the good is bad, or the bad is good. What it does is to offer for art (and life) a different – a supplementary – set of standards."[61]

The work by Venturi and his group taught us to obviate categories for beautiful and ugly. Moreover, in the case of Las Vegas, they showed how things considered absolutely ugly in daily life and in North American architecture could be raised to artistic stimuli or even iconographic models from which to learn. "The archetypal Los Angeles will be our Rome and Las Vegas our Florence; and, like the archetypal grain elevator some generations ago, the Flamingo sign will be the model to shock our sensibilities towards a new architecture."[62] The last chapter of *Learning from Las Vegas* is devoted precisely to the "Theory of Ugly and Ordinary and Related and Contrary Theories." Starting with Philip Johnson's criticism of their work as "ugly and ordinary," a criticism launched from a typically modernist stance, the postmodern theorists go on to make a cogent analysis of categories such as "ugly and beautiful" and "ordinary and original." They stress that the difference lies between seeing the work as a process, as mere material content that can also be poor and conventional, and its symbolic use, which brings new meaning to the familiar and conventional through the principles of copying and ironic allusion.

Finally, it seems that *trash* and *junk* are often multi-use labels in contemporary aesthetic judgments. In Italy, the witty columnist Natalia Aspesi criticizes her own past "radical-chic" exaltation over the trash industry, as in part does Alberto Arbasino. At the same time architect Rem Koolhaas acts as theorist for the so-called *junk-space*, and Jon Jerde, creator of the Fremont Street Experience and designer of the Bellagio, chooses as his motto: "the communal experience is a designable event."

From what has been defined as the *All-inclusive Vegaesthetic*,[63] there is still a lot to learn.

42. Las Vegas: Caesars Palace, Pool

5. Italian-Themed Resorts: Caesars Palace, the Bellagio, The Venetian – The Copies and the Originals

"The name of Italy has magic in its very syllables."
Mary Shelley

Roman Holiday

Everything started with Caesars Palace in the mid 1960s, a complex that has undergone numerous renovations and enlargements, even as we write this text. Indeed, nothing in Las Vegas is "definitive." The case of Caesars is perhaps unique, because through its transformations and stratifications, it sums up a slice, "in progress," of the passing from the "modern" style of the motels to the more elaborate theme-resort style. Comparison of photographs documenting the original buildings and decorations, the changes in following years, and the current conditions, alone represents a chapter in the history of Las Vegas architecture from the 1960s to the present time. (fig. 43)

Born from the mind of Jupiter/Jay Sarno and designed by architect Melvin Grossman, Caesars Palace became the largest, most luxurious hotel-casino on the Strip, a veritable Greco-Roman Palace in the desert. Eugene Moehring notes that,

43. Las Vegas: Caesars Palace, Panoramic View

to make his "dream" more realistic, Sarno had marble and stone brought over from Italy; to recall the Latin language, he gave the various places in the resort names ending in -um, such as the "Noshorium Coffee Shop." The theater, named "Circus Maximus," had one thousand seats – a large capacity for that time – and imitated the circular structure of the Colosseum, while waitresses in short tunics and satyrs with vine-leaf wreaths on their heads welcomed guests to "The Bacchanal" restaurant. It was like the set from a *peplum* film, or spear-and-sandal epic! (fig. 44)

And that's not all: "obsessed with the notion that oval design promoted relaxation, Sarno not only ordered an egg-shaped casino, but also repeated the elliptical theme throughout the resort's buildings and grounds."[64]

44. Rome: Piazza Navona, Fountain, Detail

Venturi took Caesars as an archetype for comparison with Rome, the Rome of monuments and ruins, of the Roman Forum with its uneven, stone-block roads, bushes, trees, statues, columns, capitals, and triumphal arches, from which Caesars obviously took inspiration. Above all, Venturi took Caesars as an urbanistic model. (fig. 45) When Venturi stated, "Las Vegas, which I learned from via the perspective of Rome" ("Acceptance Speech of the Pritzker Prize"), he meant not only that Las Vegas took inspiration from Rome, which is rather obvious, but also that through Rome we can understand Las Vegas.
(figs. 46,47)

> "Like the complex architectural accumulations of the Roman Forum, the Strip by day reads as chaos if you perceive only its forms and exclude its symbolic content. The Forum, like the Strip, was a landscape of symbols, with layers of meaning evident in the location of roads and buildings, buildings representing earlier buildings and the sculpture piled all over. Formally the Forum was an awful mess; symbolically it was a rich mix."
> Venturi, Scott Brown, and Izenour

45. Rome: Roman Forum, Silhouette

When Caesars made its appearance, it revealed the structure of a European city, built around a square to be strolled through, to the less aware American public. "Las Vegas is to the Strip what Rome is to the Piazza."[65] And many are the piazzas on a tourist's ideal "Roman Holiday" itinerary, each one with its own fountain and group of statues, and with its varied, multiple, asymmetrical, and often surprising entrances allowing for maximum pedestrian traffic (as Camillo Sitte reminded us long ago), from Piazza Navona to the Pantheon, and from the Turtle Fountain to the Trevi Fountain, where you can throw in a coin for good luck. (figs. 48-54)

> *"The romantic, the idealist, the tender-minded of any vein dies a thousand deaths in these fountains; their every dolphin is his nemesis."*
>
> *Eleanor Clark,* The Fountains of Rome, *1952*

(figs. 55-57)

But the piazza *par excellence* is St. Peter's, surrounded by, or shall we say wrapped in Bernini's colonnade. And this is precisely the model you will see in pictures of Caesars Palace in the 1960s, that of a great piazza, which initially served as a parking lot, surrounded on two sides by the symmetrical wings of the

46. Las Vegas: Caesars Palace, Exterior, Details

47. Las Vegas: Caesars Palace, Entrance to Pool Deck

48. Rome: Turtle Fountain, Taddeo Landini (1585)

49. Rome: Trevi Fountain, Nicola Salvi (1762)

50. Rome: Piazza Navona, Obelisk in the Fountain of Four Rivers, Gian Lorenzo Bernini (1651)

51. Roma: Piazza Navona, Neptune Fountain

52. Las Vegas: Caesars Palace, Forum Shops, Horse Statue

53. Rome: Piazza Navona, the Fountain of Four Rivers, Horse, Detail

54. Rome: Pantheon (27 B.C.)

55. Rome: St. Peter's Square, Bernini Colonnade, Detail (1656/67)

56. Las Vegas: Caesars Palace, Nike of Samothrace (copy) Statue and Fountain

57. Rome: Roman Forum, House of Vestals Road

colonnade, just like open arms. In the center, a long stretch of pools and fountains lined with cypresses and statues led the eye toward the *porte-cochère* of the central building, which was set back from the street. Meanwhile, on the Strip stood a sign in theme, a mix between a triumphal arch and a tempietto crowned by a tympanum, with ionic columns and, at the base, centurions replete with feathered helmets.

"Gladiators vs. boxers." From the steps of the Colosseum, the vast audiences of ancient Rome, consisting of more than 50,000 spectators, could watch the games of gladiators engaged in mortal combat, between one another and with ferocious beasts. During the reign of emperor Vespasian, it is said that almost one hundred games were held in one year. The same enthusiasm for what can be considered today's "gladiator games" – not quite as bloody, or at least usually not – has been seen in the Las Vegas rings at encounters between boxing greats from Muhammad Ali to Mike Tyson.

(figs. 58, 59)

In the 1970s, postmodern architecture provided other examples to go alongside that of Caesars, where the hedonistic aspect is evident, as is the attention paid to the exterior dimension and, above all, to the scenographic, if not cinematic, montage (in those years there was a move away from *peplum* films, considered kitsch, but in the cities, classical elements were employed as ironic, cultured quotations). This was also the case with "Piazza d'Italia" in New Orleans (1975–78), designed by Charles Moore, with its references to Rome's baroque fountains and classical column orders, which are however covered in irony by neon lights that make them a typical example of "applied decoration."[66] Could the memory of De Chirico's "Piazza d'Italia" be behind it as well?

Beyond this, however, Venturi's study from the 1970s also brought to light the aspect linked to the semiotics of objects in an urban space. With his analysis of the duck-shaped "Long Island Duckling" building as sign, he also touched on the architecture of the motels along the famous Route 66, where huge signs struck the eye immediately, while the buildings behind them were modest and architecturally unimportant, or rather, where the communication aspect was more important than the space. Las Vegas followed that model – with giant billboards that lit up in the night in the brightest neon colors, "The sign is more important than the architecture"[67] – until Caesars Palace, which still today has the biggest sign (fig. 60) (more richly decorated in stucco and gold with respect to the original). However, Caesars also introduced a decisive change that has led to the present moment in which, through the themed resort, the building becomes its own sign. Moreover, from an attention paid primarily to the exterior, to the façade, to the "shell," there has been a move to buildings whose grandiose exteriors correspond to even more imposing interiors rich with highly inventive solutions: monumental atriums, passages, forums with still and animated statue groups, fountains, gardens, greenhouses, and pools, in line with the desert-oasis model. (fig. 61) The "ha-ha!" principle of eighteenth-century tradition – the surprise and marvel provoked purposely before an artificially modified landscape – comes back in the almost infinite competition between the new themed resorts of the end of the millennium.

58. Las Vegas: Caesars Palace, Colosseum Theater

59. Rome: Colosseum, Silhouette

60. *Las Vegas: Caesars Palace, Arch-Sign*

61. *Las Vegas: Caesars Palace, Forum Shops, Group of Statues*

62. Rome: the Vittoriano, Monument to King Victor Emanuel II, (1885/1911), Giuseppe Sacconi, Detail of Columns with Angels

63. Rome: the Vittoriano, Overall Perspective View

64. Rome: the Vittoriano, Chariot

65. Las Vegas: Caesars Palace, Statue of Apollo

66. Rome: Campidoglio Square, designed by Michelangelo (1536)

Today, Caesars Palace is an inaccurate but imaginative mixture of imperial Rome and baroque luxury, much showier than that of the 1960s, and so grandiose that it far exceeds even the "wildest dreams of any Roman Pope or Emperor"; an authentic triumph – Alberto Arbasino would say – of "the more the better." And the sources of inspiration are manifold: in addition to ancient Rome, there is an eclectic mixture of Renaissance Rome and the great villas of Tivoli.[68] And we must not forget the Vittoriano, or Altar of the Fatherland dedicated to King Victor Emanuel II, whose massive structure dominates Piazza Venezia. (figs. 62-64) That monument, built between the late 1800s and the early 1900s, is also a "copy" or reinvention of classical inspiration. Not just Las Vegas exhibits fakes and forgeries.

As such, a long row of high columns, surmounted by winged and trumpet-playing angels, leads to the Caesars casino entrance, while a gilded quadriga and a circular tempietto hosting a statue of Apollo (fig. 65) greet visitors at the sides of the long moving sidewalk that takes them inside. Through its combination of epochs and of provenances, the statuary shows even more clearly the indifference to any sort of philological contextualization, and the white that dominates in the statues reflects Neoclassical influence, whereas today archaeologists stress the use of polychromy in ancient Greek and Roman sculpture: from the ancient Imperial Forums, with a line of Vestals, to the twentieth-century Foro Italico, from the Vatican Museums to the Campidoglio (figs. 66,67) – with its piazza designed by Michelangelo, the Dioscuri at the top of the stairs, and the statue of Marcus Aurelius on horseback in the center. There are even copies from the Louvre in Paris and the Uffizi in Florence: (figs. 68-73) the Nike of Samothrace, the Venus de Medici, Michelangelo's David, and the Rape of a Sabine by Giambologna (Jean de

67. Rome: Campidoglio Square, Marcus Aurelius on Horseback, (Second Century A.D.)

68. Las Vegas: Caesars Palace, Forum Shops, David (copy)

Boulogne), plus the three Graces, various other Venuses, sphinxes, and mythological chimeras, all stand triumphantly as if in a gigantic open-air museum of copies. The statue that dominates over them all is, of course, that of Caesar Augustus (not Julius Caesar, as some books report, but anyway it is still a Caesar!). (figs. 74,75) The original statue, called Augustus at Prima Porta after the place where it was found, is now located in the Vatican Museums: the copy is almost perfect, the cuirass copiously decorated with reliefs and at the base, a small statue of Cupid riding a dolphin, alluding to Venus, mythical ancestress of the Gens Iulia.[69]

The pools are worthy of the most lavish thermal baths at the villas of Tiberius or Adriano, set off by statues and tempiettos, herms and vases on slender columns, all embellished by lush plants and high jetting fountains. (fig. 76)

Caesars Palace was also the first resort to fully exploit the idea of a covered mall: the Forum was added onto the original building in 1990 by a group of architects from Marnell Corrao Associates, and enlarged in 1997. Its trompe l'oeil sky, with lights programmed to simulate the changing of time from day to night, gives an almost perfect illusion of reality. It is an air-conditioned promenade among exclusive shops and elegant restaurants hosted by "palazzos" that recall Renaissance and baroque Rome, with elaborate reliefs surmounted by rows of classical-style statues. (fig. 77) As in the Roman piazzas, open spaces and intersections are embellished with fountains and statue groups: winged horses and Tritons surround the gods that dominate the scene, from the merry Bacchus to a harsh Neptune. The latter is, however, perhaps more in harmony with the elaborate "King Neptune" costume designed for Liberace in 1984 by Michael Travis than with the mythological god of the seas. Then, all of a sudden, the statues come to life: technological miracle at the service of make believe![70]

69. Las Vegas: Caesars Palace, Rape of the Sabine (copy)

70. Las Vegas: Caesars Palace, Nike (copy)

71. Las Vegas: Caesars Palace, David and Venus (copies)

72. *Las Vegas: Caesars Palace, Three Graces*

73. *Las Vegas: Caesars Palace, Forum Shops, Caryatid*

74. Las Vegas: Caesars Palace, Statue of Caesar Augustus (copy)

75. Rome: Statue of Caesar Augustus (Octavian, 63 B.C./A.D. 14) Known as Augustus at Prima Porta, Vatican Museums (*credit: Musei Vaticani)

76. Las Vegas: Caesars Palace, Exterior with Gilt Goddess Statue

77. Las Vegas: Caesars Palace, Forum Shops, Neptune Statue

78. Las Vegas: Caesars Palace, Forum Shops, Talking Statues

79. Las Vegas: Caesars Palace, Forum Shops, Talking Statues

"Talking statues in papal Rome." (figs. 78,79) They are called "talking statues," but they are not, as in the case of Las Vegas, mechanical devices that come to life according to a specific schedule for the enjoyment of the show. Instead, they constituted a papal Rome version of modern-day graffiti. Four statues (or better, stumps of statues) served as the place where citizens, tired of impositions and abuses by the rich and powerful, posted anonymous protests, often in a heavily satirical vein. They were also called "pasquinades" after the statue of Pasquino near Piazza Navona.

The Italian Lakes: magic words!

As we mentioned, Lake Como was one of the favorite destinations on the Grand Tour. Varenna, Tremezzo, Cadenabbia, Cernobbio, and Bellagio were mandatory stops in the Baedeker of high-class tourism between the nineteenth and twentieth centuries, and they remain so today. (fig. 80)

In *Italian Hours*, Henry James compares the panorama, in his opinion artificial and "constructed" even if pleasant, to opera sets: "The pink-walled villas gleaming through their shrubberies of orange and oleander, the mountains shimmering in the hazy light like so many breasts of doves, the constant presence of the melodious Italian voice." Stendhal and Flaubert are enchanted by the views of incomparable beauty, while an inspired Henry Longfellow writes: "I ask myself 'Is this a dream?/ Will it all vanish into air?/ Is there a land of such supreme/ And perfect beauty anywhere?'"; and William D. Howells considers his visit to Lake Como as "a dream of summer." (figs. 81,82)

To recreate the dream and the enchantment, the Bellagio opened in Las Vegas in 1998, immediately signaling a new phase in the panorama of the Strip. Not only did architect Jon Jerde, defined by Steve Wynn as "the Bernini of our times," create an environment of great beauty and magnificence, but he also accented the aspect of nature, through gardens full of Mediterranean plants, flowering lavender and hydrangea bushes, and the entrance road lined with wild olive, lemon, and cypress

80. *Bellagio, Lake Como: View of the Town*

81. Bellagio, Lake Como: Villa Melzi d'Eril (1808), Dome in the Park

82. Bellagio, Lake Como: View

83. Las Vegas: Bellagio Hotel, Exterior with Fountain

84. Las Vegas: Bellagio Hotel, Entrance-Sign

trees. (figs. 83-84) The Bellagio also represents the triumph of water, with its lake (Lake Como!) and water jets that spray in time with the music, thanks to a complicated and innovative *son et lumière* system: when the water starts spouting, the jets go increasingly higher, creating fascinating choreography, while the notes of "Singin' in the Rain" or of the greatest opera hits fill the air. Thus, the greatest fountain in the world is located in one of the most desert-like cities in the United States. Steve Wynn, who has to an extent created his own personal pleasure garden on the Strip, says that "Water is at the heart of the juxtaposition between fantasy and reality on which Las Vegas subsists."[71]

A similarly complex system, though on a smaller scale, was recently employed in the Grove, an open-air mall in Los Angeles. There, the choreography consists of a street meant to recall the Los Angeles of the 1930s and 1940s, with buildings echoing a number of styles, European-flavored intersections between narrow streets, and a square sporting a dancing fountain created by WET (Water Entertainment Technology) Design of Universal City, California, the same firm that designed the fountains at the Bellagio.

And the Moors who ring the bells in the Venice Clock Tower return in the enormous carillon dominating the building which closes off the piazza, except in art deco style and more closely resembling the powerful-bodied workers that decorate Rockefeller Center in New York. (fig. 85)

> "Welcome to a place where all the world is water, and the stage is all the world."
> From the program for the Cirque du Soleil show "O" held at the Bellagio

About twenty miles from Las Vegas, there's Lake Mead, a lake with crystal-clear waters over a red rock bottom. It too is an artificial lake, formed by the Hoover Dam (a splendid art deco monument), supplying water to the city since the 1930s. Las Vegas would never have developed as it has, were it not for the great water supply coming from the Colorado River. The city owes its name, though, to the underground sources of artesian wells, used first by the Indians and then the Mormons. Indeed, Las Vegas means "the meadows," named as such by Spanish explorers who wanted to name the city after the oasis. Of the many myths which Las Vegas produces and on which it feeds, perhaps the most appealing is that of a paradise born in the desert, and the monuments to that myth are the fountains, whether outside the casinos or inside the malls. (fig. 86)

Water surrounds the façade of The Venetian with its canals; "Roman" statues are mirrored in the water at Caesars; water refreshes the Desert Passage shopping complex at the Alladin with timed artificial rain; water is the battlefield where beautiful sirens and renegade pirates confront one another in front of Treasure Island; and the incandescent lava, which erupts from the volcano in front of the Mirage, is water. The hotel pools – reserved for guests only – are often the most exclusive places, rich with lush vegetation, embellished with waterfalls and islands like the Polynesian jungle of Mandalay Bay. (figs. 87-89)

Tom Vanderbilt was right when he said that "Water, rather than neon, is dazzling tourists and selling fantasy on the modern-day Strip":[72] a sort of utopia of the American dream, a new legendary Shangri-la of the Western world. Finally, according to critic Dave Hickey, water represents purification: "Las Vegas is the place where America's puritan façade dissolves into a catholic taste for water, sin and redemption through risk-taking."[73]

In the case of the Bellagio, water is the first element that brings to mind the Italian lake country. Overall, however, reference to the original is more by suggestion than in substance. "A small moment of invented history," comments Aaron Betsky.[74] Indeed, the intention of Design Director Roger Thomas[75] was not to make the sumptuous resort a true "copy" or even a "replica," but rather to suggest a sort of subliminal effect: the magnificence of the Bellagio must recall the refined nature of the

85. Los Angeles, Calif.: The Grove, Dome with Clock

ancient villas on Lake Como, like Villa Carlotta in Tremezzo, or those later turned into luxury hotels such as Villa d'Este and Grand Hotel Villa Serbelloni. (figs. 90-94)

Las Vegas's most famous illusionist, Penn Jillette of the duo Penn & Teller, stated – though it is unknown whether he was serious or joking – "I don't know where the original Bellagio is. It's probably in Europe and very dirty." Nonetheless, the Italian Bellagio – defined by poet Shelley as "the pearl of the lake" – is truly one of the jewels of Lake Como, a destination for upper-class tourism since ancient times. Legend has it that even Pliny the Younger owned a villa there.

In an area made famous by Alessandro Manzoni, the town is located on the extreme tip of the region that separates the lake into two branches; Bellagio is surrounded by hills blanketed in plants and flowers, and its colorful houses and many villas extend along the lakeshore. Curving roads and shady staircases climb up from the lake to the top of a promontory dominated by a great park, which surrounds the other Villa Serbelloni, now home to the Rockefeller Foundation. (fig. 95) The two most important villas lie at opposite ends of the lakeshore: the first, Villa Melzi d'Eril, (fig. 96) built in Napoleonic times, has a vast park and a chapel whose small dome is recalled in the domes towering over certain buildings at the Bellagio in Las Vegas. The second villa is the Grand Hotel Villa Serbelloni, (fig. 97) with terraced gardens descending toward the lake. It is a refined, discreet hotel with the feel of antique luxury. Originally an aristocratic home, it became a hotel in 1873, and since then its halls have hosted festivities for princes and ladies, actors, and important politicians, ranging from King Farouk to Winston Churchill, Clark Gable, and John F. Kennedy.

86. Las Vegas: Caesars Palace, Detail of Sculpture behind Falls

88. Las Vegas: Bellagio Hotel, Pool (*credit: Bellagio Hotel)

87. Las Vegas: The Venetian Hotel, Doge's Palace with Canals

89. Las Vegas: Bellagio Hotel, Detail of "Village"

90. Bellagio, Lake Como: Villa Melzi d'Eril

91. Tremezzo, Lake Como: Villa Carlotta (18th Century)

92. Bellagio, Lake Como: Grand Hotel Villa Serbelloni

93. Cernobbio, Lake Como: Grand Hotel Villa d'Este, Pellegrino Pellegrini (from 1565/70)

94. Las Vegas: Bellagio Hotel, Detail of "Village" with Domes

95. Bellagio, Lake Como: View of Town with Villa Serbelloni/Rockefeller, Top Right

96. Bellagio, Lake Como: Villa Melzi d'Eril, Other Domes in the Park

97. Bellagio, Lake Como: Grand Hotel Villa Serbelloni, Detail of Garden

98. Bellagio, Lake Como: Grand Hotel Villa Serbelloni, Interior, Stairwell 1

99. Bellagio, Lake Como: Grand Hotel Villa Serbelloni, Interior, Stairwell 2

100. Las Vegas: Bellagio Hotel, Conservatory

The Grand Hotel's internal stairwell (figs. 98,99) vaguely resembles the stairwell in the greenhouse area at the Bellagio in Las Vegas, a stairwell that often serves as a backdrop in wedding photos; but instead of copying a specific villa, the resort hotel-casino takes after the town, as its name indicates. (figs.100,101) Its architect, Los Angeles native Jon Jerde, was already famous for the huge and imaginative Canal City mall, built in 1996 in Fukuoka, Japan. Jerde says he is fascinated by the atmosphere of the Italian hill towns, whose architecture, as he remarked in an interview with Frances Anderton, is made "by nobody and everybody at the same time."[76] It is precisely that shared, community atmosphere, the evanescent essence of an environment, of a magical place, that Jerde wanted to capture and reproduce in the Bellagio resort: the colorful homes of the original Bellagio are mirrored here with their terraces overflowing with cascades of flowers over the enormous pool/lake on the Strip, and shops with the best labels from Armani to Prada, from Chanel to Hermés, are included. (figs. 102-105)

101. Las Vegas: Bellagio Hotel, Detail of Village

102. Las Vegas: Bellagio Hotel, Detail of Village with Shops and Cafés

103. Las Vegas: Bellagio Hotel, Detail of Village with Shops and Cafés

104. Las Vegas: Bellagio Hotel, Detail of Village with Shops and Cafés

105. Las Vegas: Bellagio Hotel, Detail of Village with Shops and Cafés

106. Cernobbio, Lake Como: Grand Hotel Villa d'Este, Nymphaeum

107. Cernobbio, Lake Como: Grand Hotel Villa d'Este, Park

108. Cernobbio, Lake Como: Grand Hotel Villa d'Este, Park with Annex Reina d'Angleterre in the Background

On the other side of Lake Como, in the town of Cernobbio, stands the most romantic hotel in Italy and one of the most famous in the world, Villa d'Este. Just the name is enough to evoke incomparable chic. Built as a summer home for Cardinal Tolomeo Gallio, it became a favorite haunt for aristocrats and even an empress, until in 1873 it was turned into a Grand Hotel. (figs. 106,107) With frescoed halls ornate with statues and an imposing stairwell inside, the park outside hosts century-old trees and an Italian garden, grottoes, statues, and fountains. Above all, a flowery view leads a waterfall from the top of the hill down to Nymphaeum and the lake. On the opposite side from the entrance, on the lakefront, stands the annex "Reina d'Angleterre," which takes its name from an inhabitant of the villa, Caroline of Brunswick, Princess of Wales, who stayed there at length during the early 1800s. (fig. 108)

During the 1920s, the parking lot at Villa d'Este hosted luxury limousines, while rich Americans such as John Pierpont Morgan Jr. and famous Hollywood stars such as Mary Pickford were to be seen in the halls and along the statue-lined pathways in the park, especially in the sweet month of September. Still today, this is an exclusive destination. The Bellagio in Las Vegas wants to represent the same sense of place; reiterating this desire, among *fin-de-siècle* palmettes and elegant lanterns, warm pastel-colored walls and ceilings in decorative metal and glass, the shopping mall/promenade is called, with sweet promise, "Via Bellagio." (figs. 109,110)

109. Las Vegas: Bellagio Hotel, Promenade

110. Las Vegas: Bellagio Hotel, Promenade

117

The Glory of Venice

The final architectural gem is The Venetian: a true "replica" or facsimile of Venice on the lagoon, with its Renaissance flavor and exotic appeal, a bridge between two worlds and two cultures, East and West. (figs. 111,112) At The Venetian, everything seeks to reproduce authentic monuments, often on a life-size scale: original materials, precious marble, and frescoed halls so skillfully imitated that they hold up to comparison with paintings by Tintoretto, Tiepolo, and Veronese. And, to recreate the atmosphere, Venetian gondoliers sing "O sole mio," "Volare," or familiar arias from Italian operas, to tourists who let themselves go in the vicarious dream of a "renewed" and neutral-smelling lagoon. The make-believe effect is so strikingly perfect that Wayne Curtis has even hypothesized revising the dictionary, suggesting a new meaning for the term "authentic" as "something that looks as you imagine it might."[77] He furthermore proposes that, in cases such as this, the expression "authentic replica" should no longer be considered an oxymoron. Ironic paradoxes, or unsuspected truths?

111. Venice: Grand Canal, Overall View

The Venetian, however, strikes us not only for its perfect imitation, but also for its unique "difference." When looking at the Strip at night, from one of the panoramic windows in front of your resort, you cannot help but notice that the vast area it occupies is barely visible. The neon lights that characterized the post-modern phase of Las Vegas, and that still shine on many of the casino signs, have disappeared at The Venetian, replaced with the dim light of romantic lanterns. As such, The Venetian calls attention to itself for the subtraction of its sign, rather than for its imposition. (figs. 113,114)

Opened in 1999, the new resort hotel-casino took over the grounds freed by implosion of the Sands, "great lady of the Strip," and in a certain sense, it inherited its legacy. Backed by a numerous team of architects, craftsmen, workers, and specialized technicians, the fathers/patrons of The Venetian are magnate Sheldon Adelson and designer Bob Hlusak. Vice president and executive design manager at Treadway Industries, and with lengthy experience behind him in Arizona, Hollywood, and at Disney World in Florida, Hlusak tried to concentrate in The Venetian the entire catalogue of the lagoon city's architectural marvels. (figs.115,116) To translate the spirit of Venice as faithfully as possible, Hlusak and

112. Venice: Doge's Palace and St. Mark's Basilica

119

113. Las Vegas: The Venetian Hotel, Doge's Palace, View from Colonnade

his committee visited the Italian city a number of times so they could reproduce the monuments down to the smallest detail, just taking off some of the patina of time. "No property anywhere in the world has been reproduced with such authenticity and in such excruciating detail," Sheldon Adelson proudly remarked to Marian Green in an interview for *IGWB–International Gaming and Wagering Business*.[78]

Nothing is missing: there is the Palazzo Ducale, or Doge's Palace, and the Rialto Bridge, (figs. 117,118) the Campanile Tower (figs. 119-120) and the Bridge of Sighs, (figs. 121,122) the canals, and St. Mark's Square, which is however smaller than the original and lacks St. Mark's cathedral. Perhaps in the face of that masterpiece, Hlusak's mix and match didn't dare go any further. Was Massimo Cacciari – then mayor of Venice – perhaps right to be incensed and actually refuse to meet with The Venetian owner Sheldon Adelson?[79] To ask for copyright on historical places and art cities? On the other hand, it is the "extravagance" of a city like Venice, with the illusory reality of its carnival, its fragility and resistance at the same time, which have turned the city into a model city for perfect artifice, a palimpsest of memo-

114. Venice: Doge's Palace, Perspective View

ries, "a quarry for the architectural imagination," according to Barry Curtis and Claire Pajaczkowska.[80] But if centuries of rhetoric, of play on kitsch imitation or perfectly mimetic copying haven't overworked it, neither will the "authentic replica" in Las Vegas, which remains, as we have tried to explain, something else. Cacciari can sleep easy.

In the end, a substantial and historic analogy already exists between Las Vegas and la Serenissima: gambling. Indeed, in the 1700s, Venice – at least according to The Venetian's brochure – was the first city in Europe to open a casino, or better, a gaming house where only masked people could enter, open even before Baden-Baden and Wiesbaden. (figs. 123, 124) Actually, we found no confirmation for this. We do know, however, that the institution of the municipal Casino on the Lido dates back to the 1930s, just a few years after those of San Remo and Campione, and ten years before the Casino de la Vallée in Saint Vincent. Today, the Casino di Venezia continues the tradition by widening its circle of business in the field. The site on the Lido, and the winter site in Ca' Vendramin Calergi, a splendid Renaissance building with a neoclassical look on the Grand Canal – where Richard Wagner died in 1883 – have been joined by a new site on solid ground at

115. Las Vegas: The Venetian Hotel, Marciana Library's Angel

116. Venice: Angel, near Accademia Bridge

117. Venice: Rialto Bridge (1591)

118. Las Vegas: The Venetian Hotel, Rialto Bridge

119. Venice: St. Mark's Campanile Tower

120. Las Vegas: The Venetian Hotel, Campanile Tower

121. Venice: Bridge of Sighs (17th Century)

122. Las Vegas: The Venetian Hotel, Bridge of Sighs

Ca' Noghera, close to the airport, immediately nicknamed "Las Nogheras," thanks to an obvious assonance.[81] Finally, in the summer of 2001, the first foreign subsidiary casino was opened on the island of Malta. Venice offers numerous cultural opportunities, but the international conventions, art expositions, and big events such as the Film Festival represent only a part of what a tourist will find. Because Venice, it is well known, is all a monument, a piece of art and of living history, a museum *en plein air*. This notwithstanding, the entertainment factory that is the municipal casino is widening its range of activities: no longer just roulette, slot machines, and chemin de fer, but cultural events, concerts, and performances. Could it be learning from Las Vegas?

123. Venice: Vendramin-Calergi Palace (1509), Casino

124. Las Vegas: The Venetian Hotel, View with Sign

"Everything that happens in Venice has this inherent improbability, of which the gondola, floating, insubstantial, at once romantic and haunting, charming and absurd, is the symbol." (fig. 125)

Mary McCarthy

If we stand before The Venetian and begin our exploratory journey with the original Venice in mind, we will no doubt feel disoriented by the way in which the buildings are placed in relation to one another. In other analogous resorts with an urban theme, the buildings are concentrated in such a way as to almost form a single unit, on the model of the cheap souvenir snow globes – take New York–New York for example – or they are assembled according to the criteria for two-star icons on a "getaway escape" itinerary, as in the case of Paris–Las Vegas. At The Venetian, the buildings are lined up along the Strip in an order that by no means respects their "original," but that follows the logic of a set backdrop, or that puts together the pieces of a chess set in a seemingly casual manner. (figs. 126, 127) Hence, Ca' d'Oro, located on the Grand Canal, is found here beside the Doge's Palace, in turn connected by a small Bridge of Sighs to Contarini-Fasan Palace, which is found instead on the Grand Canal in front of the Santa Maria della Salute church. (figs. 128, 129) The Clock Tower faces the shrine with the Statue of Fortune, which in Venice stands atop the Customs Point. (figs. 130, 131) Finally, Rialto Bridge, normally located about halfway down the sinuous path of the Grand Canal, can be found here next to St. Mark's Campanile. The Marciana Library ends the line-up, home in Las Vegas to Madame Tussaud's Wax Museum. (figs. 132, 135)

However, if you retreat a little, with your back to the street, and face directly toward the front of the Doge's Palace, between the two high columns of St. Mark's and St. Theodore, (figs. 136, 137) while a gondola floats gently over the crystalline waters, the effect is quite surprising. (figs. 138, 139)

A sense of wonder can be experienced, an emotion almost similar to that felt by Gustav Aschenbach in the novella *Death in Venice* by Thomas Mann: when faced by the "the dazzling composition of fantastic architecture that the Republic presented to the worshipful gazes of approaching mariners,"[82] he exclaims, "only like this, by ship, from the open seas, should one arrive in the most unbelievable of all cities." What power of visual intertextuality! The same perspective is seen in a painting by Gaspar van Wittel ("View of the small Venice piazza with Palazzo Ducale and the Marciana"), exhibited in the Eighteenth-Century Room at the Doria Pamphilj Gallery in Rome. And we could list many more.

Certainly, the light most suited to Venice is probably a September or autumn light, slightly dimmed by the fog rising off the lagoon, in other words, the light of Thomas Mann's "sick" Venice, or of a "sad Venice," as a popular song croons, rather than the blinding light that hangs over the sky in Las Vegas. Anyway, the illusion is perfect for lovers of the fake. (figs. 140, 141)

"I have never been to Venice in summertime, or in festival time, nor at the time of any of the cinema and great art shows. My Venice belongs to late autumn and winter, the Venice of meager tourism, the Venetians' everyday city."

Muriel Spark

125. Venice: Gondolas

126. Venice: Ca' d'Oro (15th Century)

127. Las Vegas: The Venetian Hotel,
Ca' d'Oro

128. Venice: Contarini-Fasan Palace (1475)

129. Las Vegas: The Venetian Hotel, Contarini-Fasan Palace

130. Venice: Customs Point, Fortune Statue

131. Las Vegas: The Venetian Hotel, Fortune Statue

132. Las Vegas: The Venetian Hotel, Doge's Palace and Contarini-Fasan Palace

133. Venice: Doge's Palace, Detail

134. Las Vegas: The Venetian Hotel, Rialto Bridge with Campanile Tower

135. Venice: Marciana Library, Iacopo Sansovino (1537/88)

136. Venice: St. Mark's Column

137. Venice: St. Theodore's Column

138. Las Vegas: The Venetian Hotel, St. Mark's Column

139. Las Vegas: The Venetian Hotel, View of St. Mark's and St. Theodore's Columns

140. Las Vegas: The Venetian Hotel, Detail of Doge's Palace Columns

141. Venice: Dome between the Columns

Hlusak was a skilled foreman. He held all his collaborators to minute, even finicky precision in the attention to details. (figs. 142-145) The marble groups and balconies of Palazzo Ducale, the columns and precious tracery on the façade of Ca' d'Oro, the statues enclosing the top of the Marciana, (figs. 146-149) the frames, the angels, the capitals, the decorations on Contarini-Fasan Palace (perhaps chosen because, according to popular tradition, it was the home of Desdemona), and the omnipresent lions of St. Mark's — symbol of the Veneto city — are so "real" that they almost bring on a "suspension of disbelief." (figs. 150-152) Things change if we move from form to substance: plaster, cement, fiber glass, and plastic materials replace stone, marble, and brick; everything is technologically guided by a computer and covered with a hard layer that gives the impression of the original materials. On the other hand, as Hlusak comments, it's all a question of costs!

"Call it our Belle Epoxy."
Wayne Curtis

If we move from the exterior to the interior, its grandiosity is no doubt the most striking trait: already in the *porte-cochère* of the entranceway, where incredible limousines wait, imposing paintings hang above, while the lobby greets visitors with a circular basin, upon which stands a giant armillary sphere made of gilded metal rings, (fig. 153) held up at the base by nude busts of Naiads. The floor of the Galleria (fig. 154) shines with real marble in an almost perfect reproduction of the illusory game of the multicolored marble flooring in the Santa Maria della Salute church; (fig. 155) adding to it all are elegant columns along the sides surmounted

142. Venice: Doge's Palace, Detail

143. Venice: Doge's Palace, Detail

144. Venice: Doge's Palace, Detail

145. Venice: Doge's Palace, Detail

146. Venice: Contarini-Fasan Palace

147. Venice: Doge's Palace, Three-Light Window with St. Mark's Lion

148. Venice: St. Mark's Basilica, Detail

149. Venice: Ca' d'Oro, Detail

150. Venice: Doge's Palace, Detail, Doge with St. Mark's Lion

151. Las Vegas: The Venetian Hotel, St. Mark's Lion

152. Las Vegas: The Venetian Hotel, Detail

153. Las Vegas: The Venetian Hotel, Lobby with Armillary Sphere (*credit The Venetian Hotel)

154. Las Vegas: The Venetian Hotel, Galleria and Perspective View of
Floors   (*credit The Venetian Hotel)

155. Venice: S. Maria della Salute Church, Baldassarre Longhena, (1631/81), Interior

by gilded capitals. The dome in the lobby and the vaults and corner cells in the Galleria glow in the colors of baroque and eighteenth-century paintings that recount heroic episodes in the history of Venice and above all its triumph, just as they are represented in the halls of the Palazzo Ducale and Ca' Pesaro. (fig. 156) Skillful copies of Tintoretto and Tiepolo can be admired alongside nineteenth-century originals in the Guggenheim Hermitage Museum next door. When The Venetian opened, the two "Googs" were not yet there, and the Galleria was flanked on the external wall by elegant salons filled with sofas and armchairs, tables decorated with triumphal bouquets, and mirrors on the walls. That space was later sacrificed to make space for the Guggenheim Hermitage.

However, the most impressive reproduction is without a doubt the one decorating the grand medallion on the ceiling of the Great Hall, from which a staircase leads into the casino: *The Apotheosis of Venice* by Paolo Veronese, though deprived of its bottom end, displays its splendor in gilded frames, as part of a complex composition of other various glories and triumphs, including *The Coronation of Venice* by Jacopo Palma the Younger. In that painting, the amazement of the ladies at the balustrade, who look admiringly toward the Goddess/Venice on a throne of

156. Las Vegas: The Venetian Hotel, Lobby Dome

clouds, corresponds to that of visitors who, once past the bridge on the Strip, are immersed in their own "Venetian Experience." It is an example, in the words of Umberto Eco, in which "the American imagination wants the real thing, and to get it, it must make the absolute fake."[83]

The canals surrounding the outside of the buildings, replete with gondolas and bridges, do not intersect with the Grand Canal, whose serpentine path – like that of the original Canal Grande – thematically marks the interior shopping area. This, however, has no importance. Just like other malls, passages, forums and promenades, it is the restaurants with Italian names such as Canaletto or Zeffirino, the elegant shops, and the art galleries that attract throngs of visitors, encouraging them to lose themselves among narrow streets and tiny squares, to stroll under the porticos, or take a gondola to St. Mark's Square. Yes, at The Venetian in Las Vegas, there is not one St. Mark's Square, but two, even if the one outside the resort is – so to say – an allusion. And the square, with its restaurants and "open-air" café, its lanterns, the façades of the buildings, and a second Clock Tower, invites us to stay. We have reached our final destination, we have finally conquered this both real and virtual journey: the experience of a true Venetian "capriccio." (fig. 157)

157. Las Vegas: The Venetian Hotel, Bridges

Afterword

Over the past decade, Las Vegas has not only matured into what many have labeled as an All American City but also into firm academic terrain. Here, many of the forces that are shaping contemporary cities can be seen in stark relief and this development has received a significant amount of scholarly attention. Despite this trend, the architectural landscape of Las Vegas has not enjoyed similar attention, which is particularly interesting given that it was the discipline of architecture that first put Las Vegas on the academic map. In fact, prior to the publication of *Learning from Las Vegas: The Forgotten Symbolism of Architectural Form* in 1972, authored by architects Robert Venturi, Denise Scott Brown, and Steven Izenour, Las Vegas held little intellectual promise for most academics.

Given this context, it is important to note the burden that Giovanna Franci's work now faces: to be relatively alone in a field is often both liberating and limiting — liberating in the sense that the work's boundaries are fluid; limiting in the sense that the work may be viewed as having lost its compass. Despite this burden, Franci has taken on the task of examining the most recent iteration of thematic architecture in Las Vegas — that of the urban copy. Place-as-theme in casino design is not a new phenomenon but city-as-theme represents a more focused architectural strategy. Several new resorts, such as The Venetian, have taken symbolic imagery much more seriously than many of their predecessors; here, urban identity serves not only as a motif in the service of thematic image but also in the creation of physical spaces — particularly semi-public spaces. A case in point: Paris–Las Vegas is a collage of iconographic elements taken from the Parisian tourist itinerary crafted not as a "decorated shed" but as an "urban duck."[84] Paris–Las Vegas, in this sense, is a good urban building: it meets the street with well-articulated architecture; it has memorable elements; and it supports a functioning public plaza. The Venetian, which Franci visits in this book, operates in much the same way. This thematic trend represents for Las Vegas a significant shift that recognizes the increasing interest in urban experiences now found among the visiting public.

For Franci, this trend provides the opportunity to question traditional assumptions surrounding terms such as "fake" and "copy" within artistic and architectural circles. These terms are often loaded with implicit experiential qualities; we like to think that we can tell the difference between a copy and an original, particularly when experienced first-hand. This is why the Grand Tour provides an interesting vehicle for Franci's discussion for two inter-related reasons. First, the Grand Tour, which once served as the culmination of European and North American cultural training, held that in order to be cultured one had to know Rome, for example, by having visited Rome. Secondly, urban dimension has, in-and-of-itself, become a mark of cultural sophistication; i.e., cities must now have unique places that can be experienced and *known* in order to compete in a global marketplace in which tourism plays a major role. In other words, what these two visions hold in common is the underlying premise that cities, places, and things can be known in an *authentic* way through experience.

However, the Grand Tour was largely rooted in a particular notion of the authentic that may or may not have reflected lived experience. The Italian context, as Franci points out, illustrates this split. For many travelers, both past and present, the Italy of the time of visitation is not the Italy of interest. Rather, it is the

Italian past that feeds the desire to travel – the desire to relive history vicarious-ly through the monuments, ruins, and artifacts found in a given place. This is a desire rooted in nostalgia as much as it might be in fact. In this sense, authentic experience is called into question. The Italy of the Grand Tour was already a myth rooted not on historical artifacts per se but rather on historical imagination.

It is the role of the image that lies at the core of Franci's book – or, rather, the images of Italian places that have been copied in order to create new destinations. Italy as thematic image has taken on global proportions but nowhere so aggres-sively as in Las Vegas. Photographer Federico Zignani carefully documents this development by capturing both the picture-perfect settings found along the book's virtual tour as well as some of the details of those settings that may have been the sources from which other places have been made. In a sense, Zignani's photo-graphs catalog some of the symbolic images through which Las Vegas and various other places do communicate.

Las Vegas relies upon its ability to convey symbolic imagery and to communicate to a broad audience. Granted, economic interests dominate the imagery found in Las Vegas, and this certainly has its drawbacks. But Las Vegas is no different from many other cities in this respect; one could argue that urban images such as sky-lines are now as much a part of the global economy as is the Coca-Cola logo. In this sense, the commercial city-scape is in fact the popular landscape, and recent trends in Las Vegas architecture only reinforce this claim.

However, this is not a widely welcomed development. For British architectural theorist Neil Leach, Las Vegas represents a place of "degree-zero depth" and a city "not of architecture but the commodified sign." Such characterizations illustrate the degree to which distinctions between high and popular cultural categories continue to inform contemporary debates despite the fact that these categories rarely provide useful markers today. The claim that Las Vegas fails to register on architecture's cultural barometer must be taken seriously, precisely because such a claim aims to draw clear distinctions between a category of Architecture with a capital A, and its associated values, and that which is viewed as the popular or the commercial. Such distinctions not only limit the possibility of architecture to play a meaningful role in the lives of an increasingly diverse set of public audiences but also advertently or inadvertently to reinforce cultural divisions.

It must also be said that the theoretical framework upon which Leach's comments are premised ultimately points to the weakness of his critique. Leach builds upon the writings of French cultural theorist Jean Baudrillard, which posit the contemporary era as one in which images, particularly those tied to the workings of Western cap-ital, have supplanted all forms of reality. In this sense, there is no reality outside of the image itself and, therefore, we are left with a self-referential system that fails to hold any social promise or value. For Baudrillard, this is especially true of landscapes in which the media and advertising play a significant role. Therefore, the populism that underlies the work of Venturi and his co-authors, for example, has no place in the world-view of Baudrillard. In fact, populism for Baudrillard is antithetical to cul-tural practices. Given this background, it becomes easy to see that the theoretical framework that Leach borrows from the French philosopher simply cannot contend with a phenomenon that is at its root a popular expression.[85]

It is through the lens of the popular landscape that the Las Vegas Strip is best viewed. This is not to say that the forces at work on the Strip do not merit criti-cal engagement. Rather, the urban copy points to the growing relevance of place and of image in contemporary society and the ability of each to carry various forms of cultural meaning. The development of urban-theme-architecture in Las Vegas only reflects trends at play in many cities across the U.S. in which former industrial areas have been redeveloped and re-themed as urban lifestyle districts complete with galleries, coffee shops, and loft living. Urban imaginary has become a symbolic element within the broader category of lifestyle production, and this process often involves both real and imagined geographies, narratives, and land-scapes. In Las Vegas, therefore, the sign of Italy (The Venetian, Caesars, and Bellagio) actually carries social meaning and experiential qualities that both copy and differ from their respective original sources.

Additionally, the thematic architecture of such resorts represents a form of pop-architecture that is both inventive and original in its own right. So, the city-as-theme makes questions of authenticity no longer relevant: Las Vegas is, after all, an authentic place. Ask any visitor to Las Vegas and he or she will tell you that Las Vegas is real, fun, and here to stay. That same visitor will also tell you that he or she clearly knows the difference between Paris–Las Vegas and Paris, France, and the difference between Venice and The Venetian. But that difference is at once unimportant and central to the experience of each: difference is unimportant because the Grand Tour no longer holds the same value in the contemporary experience economy; difference is important because knowing that The Venetian is not Venice is only intensified by acknowledging the differences between the two.

And, it is the acknowledgment of the differences found on Franci's virtual grand tour that holds this book's greatest promise. This book represents not only the possibility of comparing Italy as it is found in Las Vegas with Italy itself, but also the opportunity to examine the production of urban places generally.

José Gamez
(University of North Carolina, Charlotte)

158. Venice: St. Maria del Giglio Church, Exterior, Detail

159. Venice: St. Mark's Basilica, Perspective View

160. Venice: Venetian Experience

NOTES

1   See Attilio Brilli, *Quando viaggiare era un'arte: Il romanzo del Grand Tour* (Bologna: il Mulino, 1995). In addition to the cited book, Italian scholar Attilio Brilli has dedicated numerous essays to the subject, including *Il viaggio in Italia* (Milano: Silvana, 1987).

2   *Italy Daily*, June 9/10, 2001.

3   R. Venturi, D. Scott Brown, and S. Izenour, *Learning from Las Vegas: The Forgotten Symbolism of Architectural Form*, rev. ed. (Cambridge, Mass.: MIT Press, 1977), p. 83.

4   *Ibid.,* p. xi.

5   Hal Rothman, *Neon Metropolis: How Las Vegas Started the Twenty-First Century* (New York and London: Routledge, 2002), p. xxvi.

6   Mark Weatherford, *Cult Vegas* (Las Vegas: Huntington Press, 2001).

7   Isabella Brega, *Las Vegas: La stella più luminosa del deserto* (Vercelli: Edizioni White Star, 1997).

8   This book has a different scope. Furthermore, others have already done that quite extensively: I owe much of my information to a number of more or less recent essays to which I refer anyone who would like to know more. See Ed Reid, *Las Vegas: City without Clocks* (Englewood Cliffs, N. J.: Prentice-Hall, 1961); David Spanier, *Welcome to the Pleasuredome: Inside Las Vegas* (Reno: University of Nevada Press, 1992); Susan Berman, *Lady Las Vegas: The Inside Story behind America's Neon Oasis* (Los Angeles: A&E Books, 1996); Hal K., Rothman, *Devil's Bargains: Tourism in the Twentieth-Century American West* (Lawrence: University Press of Kansas, 1998); Eugene P. Moehring, *Resort City in the Sunbelt: Las Vegas 1930–2000* (Reno: University of Nevada Press, 2000); Barbara Land and Myrick Land, *A Short History of Las Vegas* (Reno: University of Nevada Press, 1999); M. Gottdiener, Claudia C. Collins, and David R. Dickens, *Las Vegas: The Social Production of an All-American City* (Malden, Mass.: Blackwell, 1999); Sally Denton and Roger Morris, *The Money and the Power: The Making of Las Vegas and Its Hold on America* (New York: Alfred A. Knopf, 2001); Hal Rothman, *Neon Metropolis: How Las Vegas Started the Twenty-First Century* (New York and London: Routledge, 2002).

9   See Moehring, p. 29.

10 Alan Hess, *Viva Las Vegas: After-Hours Architecture* (San Francisco: Chronicle Books, 1993).

11 See Moehring., p. 82.

12 *I.D. – The Magazine of International Design,* Julia Szabo, "Floor Fetish," Sept./Oct. 1999, pp. 90–93.

13 Gottdiener, Collins, and Dickens, p.71.

14 Paul Davies, "Bright Lights, Big Money", *Contemporary* (May 2002), p. 59.

15 Tom Wolfe, *The Kandy-Kolored Tangerine-Flake Streamline Baby* (New York: Farrar, Straus & Giroux, 1965).

16 Beth Dunlop, *Building a Dream: The Art of Disney Architecture* (New York: Harry N. Abrams, 1996).

17 Moehring, p. 291.

18 *Architecture Las Vegas* I, no. 1 (December 2001).

19 Bruce Weber, "The Arts in Las Vegas," *New York Times*, 8 October 1998.

20 Rothman, *Neon Metropolis,* p. xxiii.

21 See also the Koolhaas essay in *Mutations*, Harvard Project on the City (Barcelona: ACTAR; Bordeaux: Arc en rêve centre d'architecture, 2000).

22 Kaleem Aftab, "Cinematic City," *Tate: The Art Magazine* (Spring 2001), p. 42.

23 Scott Dickensheets, "Glitter and Rust," *Architecture Las Vegas* (December 2001), p. 13.

24 Charles Gruwell, in *Hotel: Interior Structures* by Eleanor Curtis (Chichester: Wiley-Academy, 2001), p. 19.

25 Rothman, *Neon Metropolis*, p. 317.

26 Wayne Curtis, "Belle Epoxy," *Preservation* (May/June 2000).

27 Moehring, p. 49.

28 R. Venturi, "Towards a Culturally Tolerant Architecture," *Domus* (June 1999).

29 Wayne Curtis, "Belle Epoxy," p. 34.

30 See also J. Elsner and J-P. Rubiés, eds., *Voyages and Visions* (London: Reaktion Books, 1999).

31 Giulia Guarnieri, *America on My Mind: Viaggiatori italiani in America nel 20° secolo* (Ph.D. diss., University of Washington, 2002).

32 Leslie A. Fiedler, *The Return of the Vanishing American* (New York: Stein and Day, 1968).

33 Jean Baudrillard, *Amérique* (Paris: Editions Grasset & Fasquelle, 1986).

34 *Ibid.*

35 Pietro Citati, "L'isola del tesoro," in AAVV, *L'isola non trovata* (Milano: Emme Edizioni, 1982), p. 25.

36 E. Salgari, *I Robinson italiani* (Milano: Vallardi 1965) p. 161.

37 Nick Tosches, Introduction to *Literary Las Vegas: The Best Writing about America's Most Fabulous City,* ed. Mike Tronnes (New York: Henry Holt and Company, 1995), p.xvi.

38 Mark Gottdiener, *The Theming of America* (Boulder, Colo.: Westview Press, 1997), p. 3.

39 *Ibid.*, p. 38.

40 Henry James, *Italian Hours* (1909; reprint, New York: The Ecco Press, 1987).

41 Ermanno Bencivenga, *Giocare per forza: Critica della società del divertimento* (Milano: Mondadori, 1995).

42 Hillel Schwartz, *The Culture of the Copy: Striking Likenesses, Unreasonable Facsimiles* (New York: Zone Books, 1996).

43 Rothman, *Neon Metropolis,* p. 38.

44 Venturi, Scott Brown, and Izenour, p. 53.

45 Umberto Eco, *The Island of the Day Before* (London: Secker and Warburg, 1994). Umberto Eco deals specifically with the relationship between fake and authentic in the debate on postmodern narrative; see his *Postscript to The Name of the Rose* (San Diego: Harcourt Brace Jovanovich, 1984). He takes a more theoretical viewpoint, in opposition to deconstructivist strategies, in his general discourse on the "limits of interpretation"; see *The Limits of Interpretation* (Bloomington: Indiana University Press, 1990).

46 Rothman, *Neon Metropolis,* p.xiii.

47 Bruce Bégout, *Zéropolis* (Paris: Editions Allia, 2002).

48 See Gottdiener, *The Theming of America,* pp. 148–49.

49 Rothman, *Neon Metropolis,* p. xxv.

50 Mauro Calamandrei, "Giochi d'azzardo sulla cultura," *Il Sole-24 Ore,* 27 May 2001.

51 Jon Jerde, "The Revitalized City," *Tate: The Art Magazine* (Spring 2001).

52 S. Chaplin and E. Holding, "Addressing the Post-Urban: Los Angeles, Las Vegas, New York," in *The Hieroglyphics of Space: Reading and Experiencing the Modern Metropolis,* ed. Neil Leach (London, Routledge, 2002), pp. 195–96.

53 See Franco Marcoaldi, "Alla fiera della fortuna," *I viaggi di Repubblica,* 9 September 1999.

54 See Colin Rowe, *The Collage City* (Boston: Birkhouser, 1980).

55 Gottdiener, Collins, and Dickens, p. 66.

56 See G. Franci, R. Mangaroni, and E. Zago, *The Other Shore of Byzantium or the Imagination of America* (Ravenna: Longo, 1992).

57 *Roland Barthes par Roland Barthes* (Paris: Seuil, 1975).

58 Umberto Eco, *Travels in Hyperreality* (New York: Harcourt Brace Jovanovich, 1986).

59 Omar Calabrese, "Lo stile degli stilisti," in *Moda e mondanità* (Bari: Palomar Editore, 1992), p. 204.

60 Remo Ceserani, "Kitsch, Schlock, Trash, Camp, and Cult: What is Authentic in the Cultures of Post-modernity?" (in press); see also Umberto Eco, "La struttura del cattivo gusto," in *Apocalittici e integrati* (1964; reprint, Milano: Bompiani, 1985).

61 Susan Sontag, "Notes on Camp," in *A Susan Sontag Reader* (New York: Vintage Books, 1983), p. 114.

62 R. Venturi, D. Scott Brown, and S. Izenour, *Learning from Las Vegas*, p. 161.

63 Scott Dickensheets, p. 13.

64 Moehring, p. 117.

65 Venturi, Scott Brown, and Izenour, p. 18.

66 See J. M. Montaner, *Después del Movimento Moderno: Arquitectura de la seconda mitad del siglo XX* (Barcelona: Editorial Gustavo Gili, 1993); see also John Paul Russo, "Disfiguring: Art, Architecture, Religion," *New York Times Book Review*, 27 June 1993.

67 Venturi, Scott Brown, and Izenour, p. 13.

68 A. Hess, p. 84.

69 The "original statue," of uncertain date (maybe from A. D. 15, the year after the death of Augustus) is in turn a marble copy of an earlier statue in bronze: thus the chain of imitations dates back much earlier than the one at Caesars Palace in Las Vegas. Just recently, studies in course revealed that Augustus at Prima Porta was originally painted in bright colors. "A Technicolor Augustus," Agenzia Ansa commented ironically on February 8, 2003, following a conference held at the Metropolitan Museum of New York by Vatican Museum director Paolo Liverani.

70 Today, the illusion is also re-created by applying virtual reality to archeology. Skilled groups of scholars – such as those from UCLA's Cultural Virtual Reality Laboratory, directed by Bernard Frischer, in collaboration with colleagues from museums and departments in Rome and Bologna – give us the pleasure of "strolling" through ancient Rome by way of three-dimensional models generated on a computer.

71 Tom Vanderbilt, "Wet Dreams," *I.D. – The Magazine of International Design*, Sept./Oct. 1999, p. 72.

72 *Ibid.*, p. 70.

73 Quoted in Aaron Betsky, "Flaunt the City Electric," *Architecture Las Vegas* I, p. 72.

74 Aaron Betsky, "Computer Blobs, Wood Shacks and Slow Space," *Domus* (June 1999), p. 29.

75 Eleanor Curtis, *Hotel: Interior Structures*, p. 190.

76 Frances Anderton, *New York Times*, 8 October 1998.

77 Wayne Curtis, p. 19.

78 *IGWB–International Gaming and Wagering Business* (March 1999), p. 50.

79 See *La Repubblica*, 24 April 1999.

80 Barry Curtis and Claire Pajaczkowska, "Venice: Masking the Real," in *The Hieroglyphics of Space: Reading and Experiencing the Modern Metropolis*, ed. Neil Leach (London: Routledge, 2002), p. 162.

81 See Fabio Moretto, "Las Vegas sul Canal," *Panorama*, 24 October 2002; see also Laura Di Molfetta, "Gaming faces bumpy road," *IGWB* (August 2000).

82 Thomas Mann, *Death in Venice* (1913; reprint, New York: Random House, 1963).

83 Umberto Eco, *Travels in Hyperreality*.

84 I am borrowing Venturi, et al.'s terms that describe, on the one hand, the ubiquitous roadside big-box commercial building dominated by signage and, on the other hand, the roadside commercial structures that take the form of the product housed within; for a more detailed explanation of these terms, see Venturi, et al., *Learning from Las Vegas*.

85 For an in-depth discussion of the work of Jean Baudrillard, see Douglas Kellner's book, *Jean Baudrillard: From Marxism to Postmodernism and Beyond* (Stanford: Stanford University Press, 1989).

SELECTED BIBLIOGRAPHY

Almansi, Guido, and Guido Fink. *Quasi come: Parodia come letteratura/letteratura come parodia.* Milano: Bompiani, 1976.

Anderton, Frances, and John Chase. *Las Vegas.* London: Ellipsis, 1997.

Basten, Fred E., and Charles Phoenix. *Fabulous Las Vegas in the 50s.* Santa Monica, Calif.: Angel City Press, 1999.

Baudrillard, Jean. *Amérique.* Paris: Editions Grasset & Fasquelle, 1986.

Bégout, Bruce. *Zéropolis.* Paris: Editions Allia, 2002.

Bencivenga, Ermanno. *Giocare per forza: Critica della società del divertimento.* Milano: Mondadori, 1995.

Berman, Susan. *Lady Las Vegas: The Inside Story behind America's Neon Oasis.* Los Angeles: A&E Books, 1996.

Brega, Isabella. *Las Vegas: La stella più luminosa del deserto.* Vercelli: Edizioni White Star, 1997.

Brilli, Attilio. *Quando viaggiare era un'arte: Il romanzo del Grand Tour.* Bologna: il Mulino, 1995.

Cahill, Susan, ed. *Desiring Italy.* New York: Fawcett Columbine, 1997.

Calabrese, Omar. "Lo stile degli stilisti," in *Moda e mondanità.* Bari: Palomar Editore, 1992.

Casillo, Robert. "Pariahs of a Pariah Industry: Martin Scorsese's *Casino.*" In *Screening Ethnicity: Cinematographic Representations of Italian Americans in the United States,* edited by A. Camaiti Hostert and A. Julian Tamburri. Boca Raton, Fla.: Bordighera Press, 2002.

Cohen, Jean-Louis. "Urban Architecture and the Crisis of the Modern Metropolis." In *At the End of the Century: One Hundred Years of Architecture,* edited by Russell Ferguson. Los Angeles: The Museum of Contemporary Art, Los Angeles; New York: Harry N. Abrams, 1998.

Curtis, Eleanor. *Hotel: Interior Structures.* Chichester: Wiley-Academy, 2001.

Curtis, Wayne. "Belle Epoxy." *Preservation* (May/June 2000).

Denton, Sally and Roger Morris. *The Money and the Power: The Making of Las Vegas and Its Hold on America 1947-2000.* New York: Alfred A. Knopf, 2001.

de Seta, Cesare. *L'Italia del Grand Tour da Montaigne a Goethe.* Napoli: Electa, 1992.

Dunlop, Beth. *Building a Dream: The Art of Disney Architecture.* New York: Harry N. Abrams, 1996.

Eco, Umberto. *Postscript to 'The name of the Rose.'* San Diego: Harcourt Brace Jovanovich, 1983.

--. "La struttura del cattivo gusto." In *Apocalittici e integrati.* 1964. Reprint, Milano: Bompiani, 1985.

--. *Travels in Hyperreality.* San Diego: Harcourt Brace Jovanovich, 1986.

--. "Fakes and Forgeries." In *The Limits of Interpretation.* Bloomington: Indiana University Press, 1990.

--. *The Island of the Day Before.* London: Secker and Warburg, 1994.

Elsner, J., and J-P. Rubiés, eds. *Voyages and Visions.* London: Reaktion Books, 1999.

Farquharson, Alex, ed. *The Magic Hour: The Convergence of Art and Las Vegas.* Ostfildern-Ruit: Hatje Cantz; Graz: Neue Galerie, 2001.

Faure, Gabriel. *The Italian Lakes.* Boston: Hale, Cushman, and Flint, [1923?].

Fiedler, Leslie A. *The Return of the Vanishing American.* New York: Stein and Day, 1968.

Findlay, John. *People of Chance: Gambling Society from Jamestown to Las Vegas.* New York: Oxford University Press, 1986.

Franci, G., R. Mangaroni, and E. Zago. *The Other Shore of Byzantium or the Imagination of America.* Ravenna: Longo, 1992.

Gottdiener, Mark. *The Theming of America: Dreams, Visions, and Commercial Spaces.* Boulder, Colo.: Westview Press, 1997.

Gottdiener, Mark, Claudia C. Collins, and David R. Dickens. *Las Vegas. The Social Production of an All-American City.* Malden, Mass.: Blackwell, 1999.

Greenblatt, Stephen. *Marvellous Possessions: The Wonder of the New World.* Oxford: Clarendon Press, 1991.

Hancock III, Virgil. *American Byzantium: Photographs of Las Vegas.* Essay by Gregory McNamee. Albuquerque: University of New Mexico Press, 2001.

Hess, Alan. *Viva Las Vegas: After-Hours Architecture.* San Francisco: Chronicle Books, 1993.

Huguenim, Daniel, and Erich Lessing. *The Glory of Venice: Ten Centuries of Imagination and Invention.* Paris: Terrail, 1995.

James, Henry. *Italian Hours.* 1909. Reprint, New York: The Ecco Press, 1987.

Jameson, Fredric. *Postmodernism, or, The Cultural Logic of Late Capitalism.* Durham: Duke University Press, 1991.

Kellner, Douglas. *Jean Baudrillard: From Marxism to Postmodernism and Beyond.* Stanford: Stanford University Press, 1989.

Land, Barbara, and Myrick Land. *A Short History of Las Vegas.* Reno: University of Nevada Press, 1999.

Leach, Neil, ed. *The Hieroglyphics of Space: Reading and Experiencing the Modern Metropolis.* London: Routledge, 2002.

Lombardo, Agostino. *Il diavolo nel manoscritto: Saggi sulla tradizione letteraria americana.* Milano: Rizzoli, 1974.

Lyotard, Jean-Francois. *La condition postmoderne.* Paris: Les Editions de Minuit, 1979.

Mann, Thomas. *Death in Venice.* 1913. Reprint, New York: Random House, 1963.

McCarthy, Mary. *Venice Observed.* New York: Harvest/Harcourt Brace Jovanovich, 1963.

Moehring, Eugene P. *Resort City in the Sunbelt: Las Vegas 1930–2000.* Reno: University of Nevada Press, 2000.

Montaner, J. M. *Después del Movimento Moderno: Arquitectura de la seconda mitad del siglo XX.* Barcelona: Editorial Gustavo Gili, 1993.

Newton, Wayne. Foreword to *Las Vegas,* photographs by Santi Visalli. New York: Universe, 1996.

Pfister, Manfred, ed. *The Fatal Gift of Beauty: The Italies of British Travellers.* Amsterdam: Rodopi, 1996.

Reid, Ed. *Las Vegas: City without Clocks.* Englewood Cliffs, N. J.: Prentice-Hall, 1961.

Rothman, Hal K. *Devil's Bargains: Tourism in the Twentieth-Century American West.* Lawrence: University Press of Kansas, 1998.

--. *Neon Metropolis: How Las Vegas Started the Twenty-First Century.* New York and London: Routledge, 2002.

Rowe, Colin. *The Collage City.* Boston: Birkhouser, 1980.

Russo, John Paul. Review of *Disfiguring: Art, Architecture, Religion,* by Mark C. Taylor. *New York Times Book Review,* 27 June 1993.

Schwartz, Hillel. *The Culture of the Copy: Striking Likenesses, Unreasonable Facsimiles.* New York: Zone Books, 1996.

Sontag, Susan. "Notes on Camp." In *A Susan Sontag Reader.* New York: Vintage Books, 1983.

Spanier, David. *Welcome to the Pleasuredome: Inside Las Vegas.* Reno: University of Nevada Press, 1992.

Tronnes, Mike, ed. *Literary Las Vegas: The Best Writing about America's Most Fabulous City.* New York: Henry Holt and Company, 1995.

Twain, Mark. *The Innocents Abroad.* 1869. Reprint, New York: New American Library, 1966.

Vance, William L. *America's Rome.* New Haven: Yale University Press, 1989.

Venturi, Robert, Denise Scott Brown, and Steven Izenour. *Learning from Las Vegas: The Forgotten Symbolism of Architectural Form.* Rev. ed., Cambridge, Mass.: MIT Press, 1977.

Weatherford, Mark. *Cult Vegas.* Las Vegas: Huntington Press, 2001.

Wilton, Andrew, and Ilaria Bignamini, eds. *Grand Tour: The Lure of Italy in the Eighteenth-Century.* London: Tate Gallery Publishing, 1996.

Wolfe, Tom. *The Kandy-Kolored Tangerine-Flake Streamline Baby.* New York: Farrar, Straus and Giroux, 1965.